Eye *from* *the* Edge

The Llamas family Victorian home: a neighborhood gathering place, La Ideal Music Shop, barbershop, and jewelry shop on the ground floor; family home on the middle and third floors.

Eye *from* *the* Edge

A Memoir of West Oakland, California

Ruben Llamas

Earth Patch Press
Carmichael, California

First Edition 2012

Earth Patch Press | www.earthpatchpress.com

Map sketches by Jay Bishop
Jacket design by Sarah Wing
Interior design and typesetting by Williams Writing, Editing & Design

Publisher's Cataloging-in-Publication Data
Llamas, Ruben.
    Eye from the edge : a memoir of West Oakland / Ruben Llamas ; [edited by] Terry Burke Maxwell.
    p. cm.
    ISBN 978-1-885401-60-1 (Hardcover)
    Includes bibliographical references.
1. Llamas, Ruben. 2. Oakland (Calif.) – Biography. 3. Mexican Americans – California – Biography. 4. Immigrants – California – Oakland – Biography. 5. Hispanic Americans – California – Biography. 6. Mexican Americans – Social life and customs. 7. Hispanic Americans – Social life and customs. I. Maxwell, Terry Burke. II. Title.
E184.M5 L585 2012

973/.046872/0092 –dc23   2012930897

Photograph Credits
For information regarding any of the photos in this book, please contact the publisher, Earth Patch Press. All photos copyright; copying, duplicating, transferring them electronically or by any other means is forbidden unless written permission is granted from the publisher and the owner as listed below.
Page 3–5: Courtesy of Paul C. Trimble.
Page 6: Photo attributed to Tom Gray. Courtesy of Paul C. Trimble.
Page 125: Courtesy of the Museum of California at Oakland, through the gift of Guadalupe's son, Charles Hector Carlos.
All other photos are from the author's collection.

Printed in the United States of America

Earth Patch Press is an imprint of
The Maxwell Group Publishing Company
4005 Manzanita Ave Ste 6 PMB 337
Carmichael, CA 95608

First and foremost, to my wife, Anita,
who was my right hand in this endeavor.

To my three sons, Stephen, Willie, Wally, and their wives.

To all my grandchildren and great-grandchildren. I want
them to know their humble beginnings and family history.

Contents

Preface

The idea for this book began while I was doing research for my family's genealogy. The search for information about my family started with visits to West Oakland and the public library to find any history of the Mexican population from 1920 through the 1970s. To my surprise the library had very little information about this period of life and social activities. The library had little information even about the churches of Oakland. I decided to write about my life in this neighborhood.

During the years before, after, and during World War II, Oakland had a large Mexican population. The Seventh Street neighborhood, which fills my childhood memories, provided many American children with rich cultural experiences from their own Mexican ancestry and from those of the growing variety of people that moved to this western edge of California.

My dad's business put him in the heart of the Latinos' lives. I have seen and heard of a way of life that no longer exists. I have known people from both extremes of life, good and bad. I remember the emotional discussions in the barbershop where I quietly shined the customers' shoes. These men came from many countries and had differing histories. But they all had strong emotions about how they had been treated, good and bad. I heard the stories of these men, and their mothers and sisters, who came north from Mexico to work in the steel mills, foundries, shipyards, and other factories. They wanted to work and take care of their families.

With the support of the Catholic church and parochial school, the neighborhood community got used to the American way, survived WWII, and benefitted from good times after the war. The Catholic nuns taught me basic skills necessary for a solid working career. I had loyal friends, and met my wife before graduating high school. I was able to find steady jobs at modest wages and provide for my family. A solid work history, with the good work habits I developed in school, put me on the path to success. I want to share my life as an ordinary American man, and I hope that those who read this memoir will see the potential of life without the glitz but with plenty of music, friends, sports, and family.

Ruben Llamas

Acknowledgments

I would like to thank so many who encouraged me on this book, mainly:

Ceci Chevere (Cecelia Cheveres) for sharing her own memories of salsa dancing and the musical time period that meant so much to her and all of us.

Pete Escovedo for verifying information not just about his family but about the music of our West Oakland neighborhood.

Railroad historian Paul C. Trimble for his participation in selecting the appropriate pictures from his collection and for his generosity in their use on pages 3 through 6.

Charles H. Carlos, son of Guadalupe Carlos, for his time to talk about his dad, who contributed so much to our era. Also Robin Doolin and Nathan Kerr of the California Museum in Oakland for helping us attain permission for the picture of Guadalupe Carlos on stage at Sweets Ballroom, page 125.

The Family History Center, Sacramento, for its resources and helpful volunteers.

Terry Burke Maxwell for helping me write in my own words what I wanted to say.

Lydia Castro for her guidance in the use of Spanish terms. Dolores Finn for her comments about my story, and for sharing them with us.

Al Cazares for letting me keep his phone line tied up while he verified store names and other incidentals pertinent to businesses in West Oakland.

Maria San Roman for helping us organize our family pictures; Tencha Amaral for helping me correct our family names and family stories; my cousin, Ron Llamas, for comparing our family histories to verify the details.

Our good friend and onetime parish priest, Gerald Cox, author of *The Radical Peasant*, the story of Father Philipps. He gave me good advice, especially at the beginning of this endeavor.

My special St. Mary's classmate, who has made us all proud, Monsignor Anthony Valdivia, for his encouragement and guidance so I was truthful but not so truthful as to tell too much about us students when we strayed off the good path.

Ron Houseman, my old school friend, who time and again responded when I asked him to review something and who helped me remember things I had forgotten.

My old family friend, Carl "Bobo" Olson, for his model of success and the years he shared his talent with the workers nearby in Rancho Murietta.

Dolores Delgado Campbell, PhD, professor at American River College, Sacramento, for her consultation to help us better clarify California and Mexican-American history.

Our early reviewers, especially Amy Lignor, and Alma and Richard Hanson, Ron and Pat Teilh, and Ann Saibeni for their encouraging remarks and suggestions.

Facing page: Ruben and Anita at their high school prom.

PART ONE
*Looking Around
and Looking Ahead*

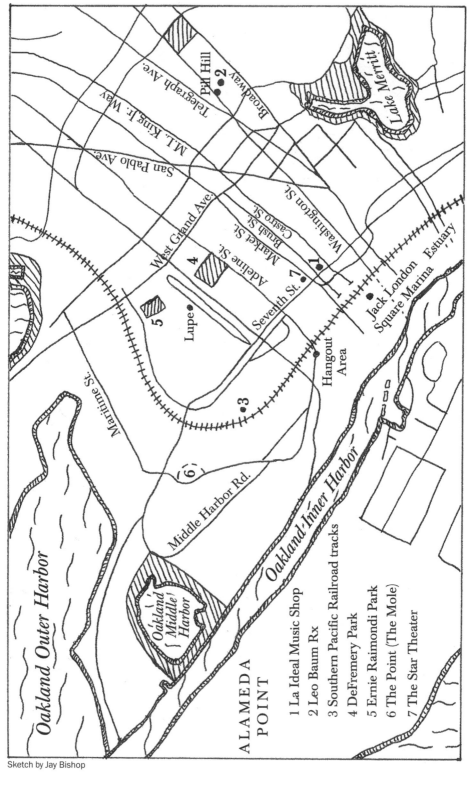

Sketch by Jay Bishop

Courtesy Paul C. Trimble

Oakland Tribune tower in the distance; passengers board Key System Transit Line, A Train, at Twelfth and Alice Streets. Interurban Key System trains ran along the lower deck on bridge railway tracks to San Francisco from 1939 to 1958.

3

Oakland's transit system included streetcars for many city routes. Some cars headed for the Oakland Mole to a ferryboat, or after 1939 to cross on the lower deck of the San Francisco Bay Bridge. Here on Broadway at Fourteenth Street, the streetcars get ready to board passengers for different city routes, early 1940s.

Before 1939 interurban trains converged on a three-mile-long pier extending over San Francisco Bay waters to connect to the system's ferryboats. Auto traffic began crossing the bridge November 12, 1936, but the bridge railway wasn't running until January 1939.

By 1941 riders preferred to drive their autos and only the Key System Transit Line remained to carry train riders on the lower deck of the San Francisco Bay Bridge.

Until April 1958, riders from Oakland transferred from ferryboats or electric trains to a San Francisco Municipal Streetcar at the Ferry Building on Market Street. Here is a B-Geary Line streetcar at the Play Land at the Beach during an off-season weekday.

ONE

Busy Boyhood

— ◆◆◆ —

My early memories of the neighborhood of my upbringing are the days before World War II. We lived at 724 Seventh Street in a grand 1800s three-story Victorian house with fancy outside wood trim. We – my parents, my three brothers, my two sisters, and myself – lived our daily lives on the second and third floors. Dad's business, La Ideal Music Shop, was on the ground floor.

The Victorian house made the music shop stand out. People passing on the sidewalk could see the activity and hear the rhythms of music. The music shop was in the middle of Dad's store. He sold 78 rpm records, plus large kitchen appliances. He sold radios and phonographs (Victor and Zenith brands). He also sold magazines, newspapers, and Spanish-language publications. And he sold jewelry. The jewelry shop, the barbershop, and the music shop were all on the ground floor. The two-chair barbershop was in the back of the store. The jewelry repair was near the front door. It was an enclosed room with large windows around a workbench facing the large window that looked out at the street.

Our house was located on Seventh Street between Brush and Castro Streets. Seventh Street was a wide street with tracks in the center for the Southern Pacific Red Train and for streetcars also. The SP Red Train station was on Seventh and Broadway.

It hauled passengers out to East Oakland and to the Oakland Mole, or the Point, as we called it, where people got off to catch the ferry to San Francisco. The SP Red Train ran faster than the streetcars. It blasted a whistle that made a scary screeching noise. You knew the train was coming! I remember well the streetcar network connecting most of Oakland's neighborhoods and the lines going to San Francisco. As a young boy I enjoyed watching the SP Red Train go by from my room on the third floor of the old house. I would hear the shrieking whistle of a streetcar and go look out the window. The rails were right outside in the middle of our street.

The neighborhood held a mix of immigrants: Germans, Italians, Jews, Gypsies, Scots, Portuguese, English, Welsh, Norwegians, Finns, French, Mexicans, Japanese, Blacks, Puerto Ricans, Irish, Filipinos, and Chinese. We had multicultural groups. Recalling the cultures I was raised with, I know we had good relations with all. It was simple: we got along. Most of the kids' fathers did labor work in the 1940s while mothers remained at home. Most families had four to six kids at home.

We kids spent a lot of time outside near the house or at the park. Nobody had money to go places or buy electronic things, so we just did a lot of playing. At the park we would play team games like baseball and basketball. Then near home we played different kinds of games. Playing marbles was popular. We would play with glass or steel marbles. The competition was fierce as we knocked the marble out of the ring because the winner kept the marble that he knocked out. We also played with a top that had a point on it that it would spin on. This was one of my favorites; it took practice to make the top spin. Also, boys and girls together played jacks, kick the can, dodge ball. And yo-yos were always popular. I was pretty good with the yo-yo. I was able to perform tricks like the Woolworth demo fellow showed us: Walk the Dog, Around the World, and the Swing were some favorites. This kind of practice helped us develop our throwing arms. I was able to buy a professional yo-yo by saving some of my newspaper money.

Playing together like we did, we just talked about and played the game. We didn't care about where anybody came from or who had what. We just had a good time. And we were able to keep ourselves busy doing these fun things. Because of the history of the area, many of us did share a similar background. Many of us were first-generation American kids. The class boundaries weren't written into laws, but they were there with the history of the neighborhoods. Jim Crow laws weren't in writing, but the cultural boundaries were around us.

For example, when a Latino went to a soda fountain counter he might get a seat. But if a white person was there, the Latino had to wait or go somewhere else. Real estate was another classic example. People of Latino descent or people of color could not buy a home in certain areas of the city. Even into the 1960s some subdivisions had rules known as CC&Rs (Covenants, Conditions, and Restrictions) that restricted the house from being sold to a person of color. The stories of what happened in the past are told to the new generation. Discrimination does leave a memory and not a good one. As a Mexican boy I heard of the past discriminations that Mexican people had to endure. These stories included shipyard experiences, tales of gold seekers not getting their share, recountings of slights caused by prejudice. Our schoolbooks don't teach about the Repatriation Act of 1930, but that episode was out-and-out discrimination.

Before the Spanish settlers arrived, Oakland was home to the Ohlone Indians. These Native Americans experienced discrimination also when the Spaniards occupied and established the Oakland area in 1797 when Mission San José was founded near today's city of Fremont. The Spanish settlers expanded to the Oakland area with pueblos and ranchos, essentially stealing more land from the Native American Indians.

My Uncle Lupe, who was really my dad's first cousin, had walked across the Mexican border with my dad. They had their legal documents in their hands. Later they often talked about Mexico's great losses in the early 1800s: Alta California, land grants like the Peraltas', and all the territories from the Treaty of Guadalupe Hidalgo, 1848. Before the War with Mexico, other states besides California had also been Mexican territory: Texas, New Mexico, Utah, Nevada, Arizona, Colorado. Uncle would come by the barbershop and somehow he would get into these discussions of past injustices. As a young boy of seven or eight, I would listen to all the men talk about how the gringo did Mexico an injustice by taking all of Mexico's northern territory. Of course, he forgot that in most of these places the Native American Indians were the first dwellers, like the Ohlones in Oakland. In those days everyone forgot them.

Now that I am in my seventies I have more time to read what happened in the past: from the Spanish conquest of the Aztec empire to the Mexican Repatriation of the 1930s, which was just like yesterday then, I see a difference. The men in the barbershop had many a discussion on these Mexican losses in America. Most of the time I would be shining shoes and would think to myself: *Why do they still have emotions on these issues? It's over. It's a different time. We are in America.* Now I understand.

World politics was also high on the list of discussions. We had other Latinos coming to the shop to get haircuts. They would add to the discussion about what the gringos did to Honduras, Cuba, Nicaragua, Bolivia, and Chile. This negative talk always left me thinking that the gringo had a big issue of control with Latinos and could not be trusted.

My thing in the barbershop was to find who wanted a shoeshine. I had two ways of shining shoes: you could sit on my shoeshine stand or I could shine while you were getting a haircut. Shining while someone was getting a haircut was always harder because a good barber will work the chair and never move himself, just moving the chair and with it my shoeshine box.

One of the events often discussed in the barbershop was the Depression of the late 1930s and how it affected the local neighborhood. My dad said that times were hard. Mexican people had no jobs in the city. Another topic was the Mexican Repatriation in the 1930s. A general fear and anxiety had spread that Mexicans were taking jobs and welfare benefits away from real Americans, and the "solution" was to get rid of the Mexicans by sending them back to Mexico.

Growing up around this environment, you absorb all these statements even if you don't understand. In this twenty-first century, we are still talking about the immigration problem. This issue is still a subject of discussion. Dad had mentioned at different times how he came north to the USA in 1923, when these events were occurring. Dad and Mom had green cards, which were legal documentation that you could be in the USA. My parents had to renew and keep these documents current to stay in the USA. They always kept their green cards with them. These weren't fake IDs. They got them at the border when they entered the USA. They showed their Mexican citizenship documents and got their green cards. In earlier times some immigrants did not possess their birth certificates or other papers. But in those days Mexicans could walk in without being asked for papers. For a long time, even after 1848 when the US claimed the territories, moving back and forth across the border was not a problem. Often Mexicans and Americans lived on both sides of the border.

The school and church we lived near, St. Mary's, were built in 1858. After first grade at Tompkins Elementary School, I attended St. Mary's School, practically carving a path along the two blocks I traveled back and forth so often. St. Mary's was an elementary school so I attended there from second grade until I graduated from eighth grade. The Holy Name Sisters managed and taught at this school. The Sisters lived in an old Victorian mansion near Lake Merritt, which was their convent.

When I was not in school or at the shop I spent a lot of time outside. Our Seventh Street neighborhood had a lot of Latino businesses on both sides of the street from Broadway to Pine Street. After school I would get my bike and search the neighborhood for all the kids I knew. One of the first areas to search was Seventh Street heading west toward the San Francisco Bay

Bridge. The street was busy with people shopping at the local markets or visiting the pool halls, bars, and restaurants. The Latinos and African Americans patronized the neighborhood shops on Seventh Street.

One of the big buildings had a group of shops on street level. These small shops were built to house small businesses and for the shop owners to live above. I would ride my bike out on the street, never on the sidewalk. Sometimes I had to scoot around parked trucks and other vehicles. I also had to watch out for the SP Red Train tracks. If your wheels caught in these tracks that were like regular railroad tracks, you were in trouble. The bike would stop you at once when its tire fell into the groove between this wider rail and the street pavement. Getting stuck didn't happen with the streetcar tracks because they used girder rails that were narrower and our balloon tires didn't get caught. Another thing I remember was the smell that filled the air along these streets. It had a machine shop aroma like the estuary below First Street by Jack London Square.

I would head over to my friend's house on Myrtle and Third Street. Danny Cheveres and I both attended first grade at Tompkins Elementary School in 1942. The school was located about one block from Adeline Street on Third Street. Then we met again in second grade. Danny and I hit it off well. We spent a lot of time together. Danny was taller than me, about two or three inches taller. He was light-skinned for a Puerto Rican and had wavy black hair that I wished I had. We spent a lot of time doing things he liked, going down to the nearby bay or the wharves along the estuary. Danny and I kept this boyhood friendship all through grade school and beyond.

I always enjoyed going to Danny's house. The Cheveres family lived in an old Victorian house with three floors. It was probably built in the 1800s. The house had been converted to flats and apartments. Three or four families with at least four or five kids in each family lived there. Danny's mom kept a clean house and a clean outside also. You walked up the stairs to get your friends.

The wooden stairs always made a creaking noise when stepped on. The front doors were colored glass on the side of the wooden door, kind of like the stained windows in church.

When I arrived at Danny's house, he would come out and we would plan our morning. Would we go down to the bay or the wharves along the estuary? Or would we ride over to the park? After we decided, we would go get the rest of the guys. We had about four or five guys that hung out together: Ron Houseman, Tony Valdivia, Albert Mammola, Danny Cheveres, and myself, Ruben Llamas. Ron was the light-skinned guy and had blonde hair. He also had a lot of freckles on his face. He stood out. We all enjoyed playing baseball, boxing, and bike riding all over the city. Even as young third graders we would just get on our bikes and head toward the repair yard located at the end of Seventh Street, the Point. We would sometimes travel down Seventh Street or take Third Street. It would not make much difference which one because they were all busy. The small shops would sometimes double-park their trucks on Third Street. When they started up their trucks, they would knock you down.

When you rode your bike with Danny you had to pedal hard. We would stop after a long stretch of bike riding, catch our breath, and talk about what we would do when we got older. Sometimes in your youth, you have dreams of what you would like to be when you grow up. We did our share of dreaming.

Sometimes our bike rides would take us to the rail yards. When we arrived at the rail yards we just looked around to see what we would find. Security in those times did not exist, or maybe wasn't important during the day. We would check out the boxcars and the locomotives. We would find sunglasses, cigarettes, lighters, coins—nothing of value, so we took it. In the boxcars you would find broken case goods, not always good or salvageable. We never stayed a long time at the yard because if you got caught they would call the police on you and that was big trouble at home. Bike rides through the streets to home were always good. The smell of the estuary was always around. By late afternoon, dockworkers were walking down the streets with their black thermoses and lunch kits. People would be sitting on the porches waiting for their dads to have dinner.

We also knew it was time to get home for dinner. It was hard to keep up with Danny. Being taller, Danny's legs made real speed so I had to push myself in riding to keep up. He rode point. You never rode double. It was a no-no. If your bike got out in the car lane you would get knocked down for sure. Sometimes we would stop at one of the Chinese corner stores to buy one-cent or five-cent candy snacks. Once we arrived back at Danny's house we would sit on the creaking stairs. His mom loved to sit on the porch. His mother, Isabel Cheveres, would always welcome you. I loved her as my second mom. That is how much I respected her. Danny also had four sisters who, at my young age, I thought were the prettiest girls in West Oakland. They were also a lot of fun. Danny's dad always sat on the bench in front of the house. Danny's dad did not look like a Latino because he was fair-skinned with red hair and blue eyes. We guys would take off to our homes for dinner. My mom did like me to be home about 5 or 6 p.m. By that time I was ready for dinner anyway.

Danny and I both stayed at St. Mary's School for the rest of our grade school education. Education at the Catholic school was reading, math, and a lot of religion. They had a lot of rules, and boy, they enforced them 100 percent! Our parents supported these rules because they wanted us kids to get the discipline and education that we needed for our futures.

The Holy Name Sisters taught at the grammar school that was associated with St. Mary's Church. The Social Service sisters in gray habits taught catechism. Father Philipps was the pastor beginning in 1936 at this parish.

We were active in most events of the school. The classes were small and the Holy Name nuns ran a tight ship. All the basics were taught. I can remember that penmanship was big. We spent a lot of time on cursive writing. English language was important, as was math and religion. We didn't do any schoolwork with the Spanish language.

The grade school was in a separate building on the lower floor. Above it was the school auditorium. We were active in school plays during the different seasons. All the classes had to participate. It was fun. I can remember starting class by reciting the Pledge of Allegiance to the American flag and then morning prayer.

One of our teachers at St. Mary's was Sister Mary Frances, a stern taskmaster with old-school ways. She taught the essential subjects and praying in class. She would have us hold our hands together with palms facing and our fingers extended. We had to make sure our palms were touching with thumbs crossed over one another in the form of a cross. If you were not complying with her instructions, she would pull your hair or whack you with her twelve-inch wooden ruler, hitting your hand and making it sting! Boy, you had to be alert in school or you got the ruler, no excuses.

I remember the spelling bees and how the entire class, thirty or forty kids, stood around the perimeter of the room. One at a time we would be commanded to spell hard words. She would not let you sit down until you learned to spell the word correctly. I believe I learned a lot in her classes. Either she was tough or I got tired of holding my hands out and getting the twelve-inch ruler whack.

The priests of the parish would often visit our classrooms. I can remember how she taught us to acknowledge the presence of Father Philipps or Father Duggan when they arrived. Sometimes we expected the priest and other times the priest would just surprise us, knocking and walking in. When he entered we all stood in unison immediately and with a loud and enthusiastic voice greeted whoever it was, saying "Good morning, Father."

Sister Mary Frances did provide a quality education to us that helped us to succeed. Being boys, we would spend time talking about Sister. The big thing was the part of her habit she wore on her head. The habit was so tight-fitting on her head we thought she was bald or had a crew cut. We never found out. I remember in her class we prayed a lot. During Lent she was into praying at the Stations of the Cross.

Our principal, Sister Mary Guadalupe, was also into using her twelve-inch ruler. She had a large wooden crucifix with metal trim hanging from her neck. She was barely five feet tall but very intimidating in her body motions. She would use either of her weapons if you misbehaved. I remember Father Philipps pulled me up once by my sideburns when I was in the schoolyard doing something stupid. The memories of how they got our attention when we were being lazy and acting up worked. I graduated grade school, and I thank the teachers for my education that made me this person I am.

The church was on the same block as the school. We put a lot of time into religion and prayer. Mass was a big thing. I helped out during Mass as an altar boy. This was an experience. I remember one priest who really liked his wine. It was something to pour wine into the gold chalice then see him drink it and get a refill. The wine was a good Napa wine. I did like the taste myself. Another thing I liked was the Latin Masses. I was learning Latin and I liked the High Masses. The funerals were very spiritual events. I liked the large candles and the holders. When I die I want the same type of candles and holders. When you served as altar boy for a funeral you got a cash tip.

The school and the church were across from a park. The houses going further west toward the Southern Pacific yard were older and mixed up with smaller homes. These houses must have been built about the 1880s–1890s to accommodate the large immigrant groups. In those days people came from all over. European Americans, Africans, Portuguese, Irish, Italian, Dutch, Mexican, Japanese, and Chinese immigrants all settled in Oakland. The population in 1860 was 1,543. In 1910 it had grown to 66,900, including many folks who moved from San Francisco, especially after the devastating earthquake of 1906.

During the 1940s before World War II, there was a theater on

Seventh Street West called the Lincoln. We used to go there or to the Rex on Saturdays, mainly because of the double features. It was a fun day. Many African Americans lived in this area where the porters for the Pullman Company owned many of the homes. In this area of Seventh Street, many African Americans owned restaurants, pool halls, liquor stores, storefront churches, and music clubs like Slim Jenkins', which I remember. The street was busy with people shopping, cars traveling the street, and streetcars and trains running. The west end of Seventh Street had a lot of restaurants with good southern food and music nightclubs such as Esther's Orbit Room. The place had many southern blues clubs, attracting the young shipyard workers, new people from the South, and locals to these hot clubs of the day.

In the 1930s and 1940s Slim Jenkins featured at his club some of the biggest names in jazz and popular music. The club was well-known among locals as a fun place for a night out. Other nightclubs in West Oakland were Sweets Ballroom and the Oakland Auditorium. The old-timers' businesses in West Oakland saw the impact of the new wartime workforce. The shipyard workers would spend their money in the neighborhood. Years later twelve city blocks of this once-booming area were demolished to make way for BART (Bay Area Rapid Transit), Interstate 880, and the Oakland Main Post Office.

Around 1949 I did a lot of bike riding with all my friends in these neighborhoods. This whole area had a multicultural environment. Riding through the streets was never a problem with the people. The Black kids knew us or knew that we lived in the same neighborhood. We played a lot of hardball – baseball at DeFremery Park and Ernie Raimondi Park. The local kids would hang out at the parks to have a baseball game or just practice. The parks were clean, the grass green, and the juvenile hall was next to DeFremery Park. You could talk with kids who were in confinement there. The exercise yard was just on the border of the park and we knew some of the guys.

This north part of Oakland was more residential than Seventh

Street. It was a neighborhood with a mixture of people. African Americans who worked for the railroad came from all over. This was especially true for the men who worked as sleeping car porters, dining car waiters, and cooks, and others who had seniority and wanted to have their home closer to their work or where the tips from the passengers were better. When the war broke out and the shipyards needed more workers, you had also African Americans from the Cotton Belt, mainly Texas and Louisiana, as well as the Okies and Arkies, moving into the established section of this area.

When an old Victorian house was converted to take in a lot of these people, it was a crowd. I can remember my friend Art's family in one of these large homes. They lived on the first floor and other families lived on the second floor or basement. Art's house, as well as other houses east of Market Street near Eighteenth Street, was close to Cathedral of St. Francis de Sales, which was demolished after the 1989 Loma Prieta earthquake.

Art had about three brothers and three sisters. His older brother was about the same age as my older brother, Mario. All of us would head over to other kids' homes on our bikes or just hang out in the neighborhood till we had to go home. I would, on Saturday for sure, shine shoes in the barbershop. Saturdays were busy for everybody. The neighborhood was busy. People were around. They came during these times to Seventh Street to shop the local merchants. Remember, the outlying areas weren't built up with big centers for shopping yet. People from North Oakland, East Oakland, Piedmont, and other areas would come downtown or to Seventh Street.

When the barbershop was slow I would go downtown to shine shoes. The sailors and the army guys were always good for a shine. I had a spot on Tenth and Broadway, in front of Crabby Joe's Big Barn. It was a great spot to shine shoes and sell newspapers. The military people always wanted to have their shoes looking good. They were on leave and most of them came downtown from all the nearby bases and from Alameda. Most of these guys drank a lot and loved the ten-cents-a-dance club above Crabby Joe's. This group was always a fun group. They spent their money. I enjoyed this corner. It was exciting to see all the action around you. The people all had something going. It was a busy time for everyone, women, men, and kids.

As a kid I saw the con men, gamblers, crooks, prostitutes, gypsies, and other people, all looking for a score. You learned to mind your own business, not to know or talk about what you had seen. If they trusted you, they would tell you a story or two of their activities. During this time I also sold papers, namely the *Oakland Tribune* and *Post Enquirer*, across the street in front of the liquor and cigar store. From the papers that sold, you received about three cents a paper. To me this was money coming in, plus the shine box money. I was on top of the world. As time passed, Joe, the owner, would have me run errands for him. I had no problems doing that because he would feed me pizza and a cola once in a while. Joe was the pizza maker during the late shift. He had a special window at the front where people would watch him prepare the dough. If he had people looking into the bar, he would show off, flipping the pizza in the air, and just put on a great show.

The inside of Crabby Joe's was something to see. They had a long bar from one end of the wall to the other. The brick pizza oven was toward the front. Across from the bar were tables where you could eat or drink; then came the dance floor. The bandstand was in back and had more light on it than a carnival stand. The big thing was the floor by the entrance and along the bar. Sawdust was all over the floor. This was typical of what I would call a joint. Also Joe had a large back room with tables for private card games. This old building would rock on the weekends. The music was popular country style—Okies and Western music—music you would hear on the radios of the 1930s and 1940s. This was music of the southern culture traditions that were being heard in Oakland with the influx of all the newcomers. There was always some fight or something going on. The bands playing at Crabby Joe's were well-known and played all up and down San Pablo

Avenue. They would draw big crowds. It was music to make all people dance and have fun.

Joe was a neat dresser. When he was not working he always dressed up. His slacks were sharp and cut well. His shirts fit neatly, and he always wore a neat sharp dress jacket. His shoes were always cleaned, shined, and casual. Joe was what I called in those days a San Francisco Sicilian Italian, with tanned skin and black wavy hair. Joe was well-known in this Broadway area of Oakland since most of the rough and tough bars and businesses were down here.

The third floor of the old building had a hotel. I would sometimes run through the third floor trying to sell the last edition of the *Oakland Tribune.* This was an experience where I learned a lot as I did this selling. At most of the rooms, people would just not answer. The ones who did answer bought a paper and got you out of their way so they could continue their business. I would sell papers till about 5 p.m. or when I knew that the people who read the paper daily had their paper. They would always have the right amount, for they would fold it and put it under their arms like it was worth a hundred-dollar bill. They would tell you about the paper not being in order the next time they came by. The job of the paperboy was to assemble the paper in sequence and sharply folded.

While I was in the area I would go over to Fosters' Restaurant. I know this place was not like the other places. They made a lot of sandwiches. The cream puffs and pies were great. The food was displayed in small compartments. You selected what you wanted out of these compartments that had doors. It was all self-service. You paid a cashier, then sat down at the round Formica and chrome tables. I sold the later paper here. When I was gone from my corner I would put up a cigar box for customers to drop monies off for their papers. I never had trouble with people taking my money.

About 5 to 5:30 p.m. Radio, the newspaper collection man, would come by to collect the newspaper money with his REO truck, a green panel truck with two doors, a double door in back, and no seat belts. Radio was about five foot six, maybe a Mexican or Italian. He had small facial features, big eyes, a great sincere smile, and he enjoyed laughing. He would pick up all the corner boys starting at Ninth Street all the way to Grand Avenue North, going up Broadway, next coming south on Washington. He would count your unsold papers and pay you off. While driving, Radio was a talker. He loved baseball. Radio was a good man. Once he gave all the kids a ride in his green REO panel truck to see an Oaks ballgame in Emeryville. The Oaks were Oakland's minor league baseball team.

After we were dropped off I would go home, visit the shop to see what was going on, then go upstairs to see my mom and get something to eat. If the timing were right, I would get my bike and search out my friends in the neighborhood. I would, by this time of day, go to Jefferson Park to see if any kind of game was going on.

Across the street from Jefferson Park, St. Mary's Church and School made a strong presence. Under the grade school they had a basement where they put in pool tables and a boxing ring to keep us boys busy. Father Duggan did this, and he had other programs to keep the young boys busy and away from the neighborhood pachuco gangs that were around our section of West Oakland. If no one was around I would then ride to Danny's house on Myrtle Street. In the evening the wind really blew the estuary smell throughout the neighborhood. I could hear the ship and train horns on my route to Danny's house on Third Street. Once in a while I would go down by the railroad tracks and follow them to Myrtle Street since the track went right to the Southern Pacific yard at the Point.

Sometimes the guys were outside their houses. If not I just left for home to get ready for school or do some homework. At home about the only thing to do was listen to the radio. We had no TVs at that time. Friday and Saturday were busy days in the barbershop and music store. I shined a lot of shoes on the busy days. I was growing in these times, and I learned a lot about shoes.

Sometimes I would go downtown to watch the Black guys shine shoes. They had a storefront on Broadway and Tenth. The small shop had four guys working it, and four stands with a lot of blues music playing. They would let me watch them and learn how to prepare the shoe for a great shine. They had a special wash for the leather. They applied the smooth-smelling shoe wax with their fingers and snapped the cotton shine rag, all in a rhythm of applying it. With the music blaring, the talking going on, it all flowed with the movement of the shiner's body. It was an art in itself and great to watch. I would take their style of shine back to the barbershop and do my customers while snapping that rag like the pros. To this day I still have my red shoeshine box and enjoy the smell of the shoe paste we used to make those shoes sparkle.

Some Saturdays the men's discussions shared and compared the history of their countries of origin, such as Mexico, Cuba, Chile, Guatemala, Honduras, El Salvador, Colombia, and Nicaragua. The history and cultures of all these men were interesting. I enjoyed hearing of Mexico and the Aztecs. The men talked of how the Spanish influenced each of these countries. The Spaniards conquered the Aztecs of Mexico in the early sixteenth century. The Aztecs had a great empire in Mexico City with pyramids and palaces, zoos and libraries, that were similar to Egypt's. Montezuma, the ruler at the time, had a large army. Cortés had an army of only 350 men and brought with him new diseases that killed a lot of Indians. The Aztecs had never had these European diseases. The story of the Aztecs is part of the history of the Americas and has always been an interest to me, but I don't remember learning about them in school. At St. Mary's School we learned about the history of the United States of America and the Catholic religion. This was basic in these times. And that's the way it was.

The men all had a story of their country and how the Spaniards exploited their country. These men that came in to see and talk with my dad and their friends were locals. They worked at foundries, at the shipyard, and as dockworkers at the local terminals. I would just listen to them and see the excitement in their discussion. I began to understand the conflicts between the Latino and the gringo cultures. The men would drink Four Roses whiskey or beer, then leave for the night. They were always dressed up so I knew that home was not their destination. I am sure of this.

Some of the Saturdays before working in my dad's shop, I would play ball at Jefferson Square Park. Baseball was my favorite sport. I played any position they gave me. I always enjoyed the game. Some of the guys played daily, and they were good. Saturday morning during the summer we played in a city league. The police department organized these games for all the kids in West Oakland. They had an old paddy wagon. They would pick us up at Jefferson Square Park and take us out to the city park in Oakland. We played all the teams. Then at the end of the season you played the City Best. It was fun. We met a lot of kids from the other parts of Oakland, mostly ages twelve and thirteen. We never had any problems with the different multicultural groups. I believe we all understood that we came from different and tough neighborhoods so why get an attitude. We would just fight it out. Some of the boys were good players. They also liked a good fight and that did happen once in a while. If you came from West Oakland –Seventh Street, they seemed to leave you alone. Our Seventh Street in West Oakland had a bad reputation during these times.

Ruben and his siblings and cousins during World War II: Eva and Mario
(back), Ruben, Alma (cousin), Martha (cousin), and George (front).

Family event at the Seventh Street house; Ruben is next to Victor with flute.

25

Ruben's old red shoeshine box, still looking good.

Radio, the newspaper collection man, with Ruben's brothers George and Victor and sister Juanita, and a friend.

A typical class at St. Mary's School, West Oakland, 1948; priest at left: Father John Ralph Duggan; center, Pastor Charles Philipps; right: Father Luis Almendares.

The library at St. Mary's School, 1947, and some of Ruben's classmates.

Danny Cheveres Jr. gets a haircut from Ruben (striped shirt) with help from his dad (holding him).

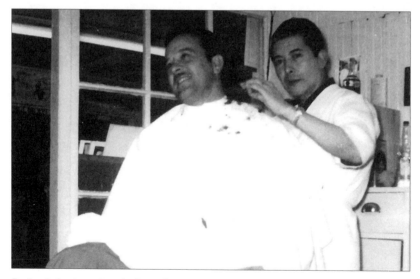

Pedro Infante gets a haircut from Ruben's dad, Emilio Llamas.

TWO

Eyes . . . and Ears

During the period right after the war (1946–1949) you could see the neighborhood changing. Some of our school-age friends' families were moving out of West Oakland to the outlying areas such as North Oakland, Fremont, and Walnut Creek. Oakland was changing. Also the end of the war left a lot of people without the good jobs at the shipyards. The city was closing down the old housing projects that housed many African Americans, as well as the Okies and Arkies. So Seventh Street started to lose more of its luster. I was a kid. I did not realize the social changes going on at this time. The old Oakland was becoming much more distrustful of the people in the area and the events going on, starting around 1946.

I remember my older brother Mario and his friends from West Oakland talking about the early 1940s and the police. They had a distrust of the police. They would say, "Don't get smart with them because they do not like Mexicans." They said, "Once they got you into the elevator they will stop it and beat you up." The other thing I heard was "Never go to Arizona. They hang Mexicans." I believe all this negative talk and mistrust might have come from events and clashes dating back to the Mexican Repatriation of the 1930s and moving forward to the 1943 Zoot Suit Riots and pachuco crackdowns in Los Angeles and Oakland.

I have mentioned how I heard in the barbershop my Uncle Lupe from Jalisco talk about the Mexican Repatriation in the 1930s. He knew a lot about the history of events in Mexico and California. I remember a trip with Uncle Lupe, traveling with him to a ranch on Highway 99 heading south from Oakland to Livingston. He knew farmers or people that worked the land as well as some of the farmers who managed them. I can still see him, stopping on the dusty road and starting to pick three huge peaches. They were cling peaches, the best kind. He told me to get out of the car and help him, which I did. There was no farmer in sight. We had nobody to stop us. I thought he must know the farmer. I later told Mom about it, and she said Uncle Lupe was not over our history, that Mexico lost California and that our Mexican Californians had to go to Mexico during the Repatriation, as they called it.

This 1930s Repatriation occurred during the Depression, when the country had record unemployment and hunger, and people had many frustrations. Americans were reeling from the economic blow of this Depression. They found a scapegoat: the Mexican community. Anti-Mexican activity and prejudice was all around. People blamed the Mexicans for taking the jobs of Americans. Immigration and deportation laws were enacted to restrict immigration and to get rid of people. Deportation and repatriation roundups picked up the unwanted Mexicans. Roundups swept all of the USA. Mexicans that had been here for many years stood their ground. They organized to stop this anti-Mexican hysteria and to end the deportations. This period was rough for the people: no job, no income. They only had their neighborhoods to help them through this difficult time. The Mexican government could not help them. It was still trying to recover from the Revolution of 1910, which had lasted for years. This roundup of Mexicans, plus many other anti-Mexican events,

I believe, left Uncle Lupe with a bitter emotion, and it would come out in his discussions years later.

Mom and Dad helped people and lived through this Depression and the Repatriation. Dad had his barbershop and worked as a small shop owner. People in the neighborhood took in boarders or family members and rented rooms to help pay the expenses of living. I believe people helped each other and they worked at labor jobs to get by. I know they did not ask for any social help or welfare. They took care of themselves. In the late 1920s through 1930s most Latinos in our neighborhood worked the railroads, steel foundries, shipyards, warehouses, terminal ships, and auto companies, and for labor contractors. Many people in the late 1930s and early 1940s became entrepreneurs, willing to try something to improve themselves. Our parents made sure that we got a good education, that we could read well and get ahead in life by learning to respect all people. They worked hard to improve their life and ours.

The neighborhood in the late 1920s through the 1940s had many Mexicans, South Americans, Central Americans, and people from other Spanish-speaking countries. Some of these folks started their own businesses and opened stores in the area where they could attract people from their own culture. I would say the boundaries would be Broadway at Seventh Street west to Market Street and Jack London Square north to MacArthur Boulevard. Some of the businesses that were around my dad's shop helped draw people to Seventh Street. Also, we were only one block away from St. Mary's Church on Seventh and Jefferson, built in 1853.

Señora Consuelo Cobian opened her store, naming it Mi Rancho. This Mexican store sold *pan*, tortillas made right there, and masa for tamales. Her store was located in the old Southern Pacific Train Terminal. Señora Consuelo Cobian was the owner and manager. This was the first full-line Mexican grocery store in the Bay Area. Consuelo was also a broadcaster for a local radio station. Señora Cobian lived by Lake Merritt on Euclid Avenue, an upper-class neighborhood.

One of the many bars on Seventh Street was an old bar on the corner of Seventh and Clay. Mexicali Rose was one of the first Latino bars. *Don* Luis was the owner. You could not miss this bar. It looked like an old adobe building, something you see in an old Alamo scene. It was painted a flat dull green. In the old days of the war this place was very busy. People from all over came here. During the late 1950s we had a lot of people from Berkeley, Alameda, Emeryville, Piedmont, and San Leandro come to West Oakland and Seventh Street Latino restaurants and bars.

On Seventh Street West, we had the Star Theater at Market Street and a few blocks down the road we would go to the Lincoln Theater. These theaters showed the newest films from Mexico as well as American movies in English. Close to the Star Theater, on the Seventh Street corner, was a large Italian bar named Old Corner. It was also a busy place, active with the neighborhood social activities. We also had a great Mexican restaurant called the Jalisco Café. The owners were *los señores* Juan y Cruz Valdivia. The neighborhood people, the braceros, and the gringos all liked to eat there. The Valdivias' son, Antonio Armando, my school friend, became a Roman Catholic priest and then monsignor. Not bad for a West Oakland boy.

We also had a drugstore on Eighth and Washington Streets called La Botica Mexicana. The owner was Ray Dami. Ray's wife spoke to the clients in Spanish and was a big help to her husband. This store sold lots of herbs that Mexican people use, including herbs for medical purposes. Many of the old-timers liked this store and knew how to use this kind of medicine. Another Mexican business was the restaurant La Enchilada Shop. This shop was owned by *la señora* Dominquita Velasco. It was popular also with the gringos.

Another store in our neighborhood was La Borinqueña. The owner was Adriano Velasquez and his wife Rosa Lopez Velasquez. They also handled Mexican goods and made great tamales and *pan dulce*. Guadalupe Carlos, an important person for our neighborhood, was related to the people of La Borinqueña.

Guadalupe owned the franchise for the Sunday *tardeadas* (afternoon dances) at Sweets Ballroom. They brought many a good dance band to Oakland from Mexico. Latinos from neighborhoods all over the Bay Area would attend these dances. It was a gathering place for the Latinos. They would come from Decoto, Russell City, San Jose, Hayward, West Berkeley, East Oakland (Jingletown), and West Oakland.

During the 1940s to 1950s my dad would have my brother Mario go to Sweets Ballroom and the Star Theater to sell Mexican songbooks of any band or entertainers that were performing. I would not help Mario until later, when I became of age to be out selling. I know my brother saw many things in these events. You can be surprised what people do when they are out having a good time and letting their hair down. I know I saw many things.

Groups of pachucos during this time also attended the *tardeadas.* They attended with their girlfriends, who had their own clothes styles and hairstyles. The zoot suiter was in this subculture. Both pachucos and zoot suiters had bad reputations because on June 11, 1943, the Zoot Suit Riots in Los Angeles left the Mexicans with a stigma or a bad feeling that we were all part of this culture. This first generation of young Mexicans who were coming out were not like their working class parents who emigrated from Mexico to the cities in California.

In the late 1930s through late 1940s people would describe Mexican Americans as pachucos. The pachucos had a certain style. They also had a tattoo of a crosslike symbol between their thumb and forefinger. For generations to follow to this day, American teens took on the gang clothing as their fad. We now see long T-shirts and low pants exposing shorts. I guess gangs from the 1930s and 1940s in Oakland neighborhoods are still around.

Seventh Street also had some pool halls, a couple of laundries run by the Chinese, the Jewish secondhand stores, a white truck factory, Lozano shoe repair, other barbershops, hamburger joints owned by Greek families, and African American jazz clubs. Across the street from my dad's shop we had a creamery. Down the street on the same side as our shop was an auto mechanic. The creamery attracted lots of bike riders. By this I mean the real bike riders, the motorcycle riders. Through the years we'd get a few crowds because the creamery was across the street from the auto repair shop. So the riders could relax at the creamery, visit the music shop and pool halls, get their laundry done, and have their motorcycle repaired. Some of these fellows were okay, but this group did have its ups and downs. When some of the younger fellows got together, naturally they had some skirmishes. So it was not a place you went to when a bunch of motorcycles were parked outside. But most of the time they were just enjoying everything that our street had to offer, especially good music, good ice cream, a good mechanic, and good friends, just like everyone else.

World War II changed the racial and ethnic minorities of the neighborhoods. People wanted a change. They did not want the same level of acceptance that was good enough for their parents. The war effort brought change and opportunity. Jobs in the war plants gave more exposure to other people, and money to do things and have new experiences. My brother Mario would say that sometimes the different groups would join together if there would be trouble. I remember the West Berkeley guys. East Oakland and West Oakland guys would join to fight with the outlying guys from the smaller towns in the farming areas. The Mexican braceros were not accepted by us guys in the city. They could not fit in fast enough to what the city guys were experiencing. Besides, many of them were mainly interested in earning some money to send to their families back in Mexico. So they never seemed to be Americanized. That's just the way it was.

I can remember many guys, in gangs or not, who came to Dad's shop. I recall people coming to Dad's shop to buy huaraches, sandals from Mexico. The fellows would add another sole to the sandal. Then they dyed it to give the appearance of a one-inch-thick sole. The hairstyle for boys was the Hollywood style, cut rather longer than other boys', combed back with a ducktail down the back and a curl in the front. Flat tops were also favorites with this Hollywood cut. Only the Hollywood barbershop owner, Phil Pino, really knew how to cut this way.

I remember buying Florsheim Cordova shoes, and adding one-inch soles and heels to look cool like the rest of the guys. Girls set their hair with bobby pins and wore a white cloth diaper turban-style, along with Levi's jeans and a man's white dress shirt with the shirttail hanging out. Throughout the USA all boys and girls took to this dress in some fashion. My dad's shop continued to sell a lot of the huaraches, jewelry, and Hollywood haircuts.

In the early 1940s the local guys and gals formed their own gang activity. We kids saw them on the streets, at church, and at social events. At this time many Oakland police had no respect for West Oakland Mexicans. So social problems still remained with the Latino people. In my observation the pachucos stood up to authority, which in turn labeled them as troublemakers. In the 1940s you knew that city hall had the power and would use it on you to keep you in place. Marijuana was a problem. Some of the kids I remember got into a lot of trouble and were sent to juvenile hall next to DeFremery Park or to Santa Rita in Pleasanton and eventually ended up in the prison system with all its problems.

After the war, in the later 1940s, these guys did come back to the neighborhood, but they were changed guys with a big chip on their shoulder. The changes were like the neighborhood changing, the society changing. The church at St. Mary's had a priest named Father Duggan who worked hard to help all the kids keep away from the new gangs forming throughout Oakland. Our West Oakland neighborhood was not like it used to be. The first generation of good guys and bad guys were not like the old-timers who were respectable people. The youth wanted to be accepted without prejudice. The saying "Do not go past Lake Merritt to East Oakland" was no longer in effect. This meant that the youth could go out to the different areas of the city. A lot of my friends lived in the projects that were built in the late 1930s to house all the people coming to the East Bay to work the shipyards, the braceros and other war transplants. The projects had the look of a square box with windows, all boxed in like egg crates. We had them in West Oakland – Campbell Village, Harbor Homes over the Adeline Bridge, and High Street in East Oakland.

I am an old-timer. I remember different ethnic and racial groups living alongside one another in the predominantly single-family homes. Most of the people owned their homes, and they or their families had been living in them for some time. The community was multicultural. We did not have the racial fights of today. The African Americans from the south, the Okies, and the Arkies had to learn how to live among other groups of ethnic peoples, since now they enjoyed a new lifestyle with no restriction compared to the way some of them were brought up. Most of the groups stayed in their local neighborhoods and had the satisfaction of living in a pretty-well settled neighborhood. West Oakland in the 1940s was a self-sufficient neighborhood. All the migrants from other parts of America and the immigrants from other countries had their own little sub-neighborhoods where they did business within their group. At this time most everyone accepted their place in society, at least until they could move to another area completely.

During the late 1940s I was about twelve years old. My dad's brother, Jesus Llamas, had a jewelry and watch repair shop, Joyería y Relojería Mexicana, at 528 Seventh Street. He came to the United States in 1923 at age six, traveling through Brownsville, Texas, with my grandmother and my dad. Uncle Jess (Jesus) was a tall man with a light complexion and wavy hair. He was about five foot eleven or six feet tall. Uncle Jess was outgoing and fun to be around, easygoing and full of life. He would give us rides on his old three-wheel motorcycle. Just like my dad, he also was a barber. He worked at his shop at 528 Seventh Street and my dad's shop at 724 Seventh Street. Uncle Jess had a good business. Like my dad, he was known in the Mexican community. I say more about my Uncle Jess in the part about my family history.

The cluster of migrants and immigrants was diverse: African Americans, Portuguese, Greeks, Chinese, Japanese, Italians,

Serbians, Irish, and Mexicans (Latinos). The groups tended to cluster by country of origin. The section between Castro, Adeline, Market, and Third Street was the Italian area. We called Kirkham Street "Tin Can Alley" because most of the men worked for the local scavenger company. Greeks lived along the railroad tracks and operated businesses on Seventh Street. Portuguese lived near St. Joseph's Church, where the Salesian priests were in charge, at Seventh and Chestnut Street.

During the 1920s to 1940s it seemed that each group had their own social clubs, grocery stores, cafés, bakeries, meat markets, fish markets, delis, produce stores, ice man, cheese man, milkman, and metal man. You could hear the clip-clop, clip-clop of the metal man's horses on the paved street. These groups also had fraternal lodges where they would meet and have get-togethers, dinners, and other events where they raised money for the needy. They followed their own generation's old-country traditions and values. In different seasons they would carry their native customs to the streets.

West Oakland Street would be active with these parades. The Portuguese celebrated Pentecost with their *festa* in honor of the Holy Ghost. Italians also had a procession. Greeks held candlelight processions around Tenth and Brush Streets following Good Friday services. In later years the Mexicans celebrated the Christmas Posadas with figures of Joseph and Mary going door to door seeking shelter. The Knights of Saint Peter Claver, who were mainly the African Americans, paraded around the church.

Saint Mary's had a large group of immigrants that were of the Catholic faith, so we saw many different customs. Someone or some group was always having a party or dance in the auditorium. We kids always had something to do at night, just hanging out and watching what was going on. Father Philipps had three assistant priests that I remember very well. They were always active with the kids and the people of the parish. They were Father Gerald F. Cox, John Duggan, and Luis Almendares from Nicaragua. Father Almendares worked closely with the Spanish-speaking cultures of the neighborhoods. He was a good speaker with a fine speaking voice that made him popular with the Spanish-speaking Catholics. He conducted a religious radio program. He was five foot eight and had a fast-paced walk with a lot of energy. I remember seeing him around West Oakland. He stopped at my dad's La Ideal Music Shop at different times to talk.

The only other Nicaraguan that I remember was a friend of my dad's. His name was Felipe. He was also my sister's godfather. He was a true citizen of Nicaragua. I heard him speak in the barbershop of all the turmoil in his country. Felipe had a nephew who lived in Nicaragua, and Felipe was helping him through school. Felipe worked in one of the local canneries. Felipe would eat at our house and visit most often on Sunday with Dad and Mom. Dad once said that Felipe was living in a room in a hotel on Broadway Street so he could save money to send to his nephew.

The church was lucky to have a pastor like Father Charles Philipps. He cared for the parish people. He was behind his priests in helping us all to have a better life and education. Father Duggan was an inspiration to all the kids in the neighborhood. I cannot write enough about him. He worked with the groups of kids who were poor, and he kept us from the gang element. After school Danny and our friends spent time at the clubhouse under the school, in the large basement that Father Duggan and a group of volunteers dug out. All the neighborhood kids would hang out here, practicing in a full-size boxing ring and playing at the pool tables. This multicultural neighborhood had a place to keep all of us busy, which kept us away from gangs.

Father Duggan had us join teams that played other schools in West Oakland: basketball, football, and my favorite, baseball. The teams were Market Street, Auditorium Village, Madison Square, St. Mary's, Linden Street, and Grove Street. I played, but I never was a special player. Some of the kids had amazing skill and were good players. We played at Fifty-Ninth and Shattuck, Ernie Raimondi Field at Eighth and Wood Street, DeFremery Park (across from the juvenile hall), Eighteenth and Poplar, Jefferson Park, the

Auditorium Park, and other parks. The Oakland Police League was a lot of fun. The Oakland Police League worked to get teams together from all the neighborhoods. Father Duggan put us into the league. Riding in the paddy wagon is a fun memory. The older boys of the neighborhood had a more professional group of players. Father Duggan's donors got the players spiked baseball shoes and uniforms.

Boxing was big at this time. Father Duggan had the top boxing team. I never joined this team. Most of the guys tried out for it but only the tougher guys made it. Some of my friends were good street fighters and the kids in the neighborhood knew it. The true boxers had accomplished boxing coaches. Father Duggan had a coach by the name of Jimmy Delgadillo. He was a top boxer. They trained for the matches at the auditorium above the grade school. Boxing matches were held on Friday nights. Boxing was big during this period of the late 1940s and early 1950s. Everybody turned out for the events. It was an exciting time. The nights that had boxing matches kept me occupied. Sometimes Danny and our friends would go with me, but after they got their cars Friday night was a good night to have a date.

I remember one night they had been training a Puerto Rican kid named Reymundo, who lived on Seventh and Clay Streets next to the Mexicali Rose Café on Seventh Street. He would ride with us once in a while. He was very strong and had a strong character. He was a boxer. He stood about five feet five inches. They put him into the ring with a guy that looked tall, maybe five foot nine, and built slightly better than Reymundo. Reymundo took a beating each round. I could not believe that he would last to the sixth round. He came out each time and gave this guy all he had and found more in himself. The crowd was excited, loaded, and wanted him to win. God must have been looking out for him that night, because Reymundo knocked his opponent out. He won but he took a beating. It's the fight that I will always remember.

Father Philipps' Sunshine Camp near the Russian River was another program for the kids from the neighborhood. Boys got two weeks, and then girls got their two weeks at a different time. Father Philipps needed help from others to support the camp. (Upon reading *The Radical Peasant* by Father Gerald F. Cox, one of the St. Mary's priests in the 1950s, I discovered that a family friend of my wife and myself had helped Father Philipps' camp.)

The friend I speak of was Carl "BoBo" Olson, a middleweight champion at the time. Bobo came to the Oakland Auditorium for a professional fight and donated his prize fight winnings for the support of the Sunshine Camp. This fight had a full crowd. Bobo was a popular boxer. My Uncle John Garcia, who had a barbershop on Twenty-Third Avenue, would cut Bobo's hair. Carl was a true gentleman. Carl was my friend, and I always enjoyed his company when he came to see me. He gave me a personal picture that I value with a lot of respect. It has Max Baer, Joe Louis, and Carl "BoBo" Olson. (I say more about Bobo in Part Two.) These great fighters of the 1950s had a lot of heart. These fighters had character, honesty, respect, integrity, and love of being great Americans.

Father Philipps' Sunshine Camp was for all the poor kids in the neighborhood: white, Asian, Black, and red, all could go. The camp, I heard, was great. My friends would come back saying what a great time they had. The kids would assemble at the school. They rode up to Russian River Camp in an open truck loaded with bags. Boy, how things have changed. You can never have an open truck loaded with a bunch of kids and adults on the highways today. The seminarians acted as counselors, leading the activities of swimming, campfires, and singing songs. Any kid in West Oakland who attended this camp will tell you what a good memory it was.

During the years we were growing up, from ages twelve to seventeen, there were many changes going on in the city. Once Danny and I were thinking back on all the good times we had with our small group of friends in West Oakland. We talked of the bike rides we took, for example, to Lake Temescal near the tunnel going into Orinda or through the Posey Tube to Alameda.

One time we were riding double when I caught my foot in the front wheel and we almost landed in the car lane. Never ride the handlebars.

We talked of the time playing in St. Mary's schoolyard at night with our BB rifles. We were running and trying to shoot each other at the same time. Danny shot me in the eye and the BB embedded itself in the corner. The spot of blood in my eye was so massive you could not see the BB. But I could sure feel it; it hurt like blazes! Danny felt bad. I told him I would tell my parents that we were playing basketball and I got poked in the eye. My parents accepted that, and Danny was happy because neither of us got into trouble. I was okay with that. I did not want my good friend to get into trouble. It did not bother me that much. Years later, when I was working on Pill Hill, I showed my eye to one of the doctors I had come to know. The eye had accumulated dark matter in the corner of my eye; it was the BB! The doctor took it out after all those years. I kept the BB and the X-ray to show my kids how you can get hurt with a BB rifle.

We also talked about taking the electric train across the Bay Bridge to San Francisco. We would catch the Key System A train on Twelfth Street in Oakland. The train would drop us off in downtown San Francisco. These trips we would usually do on Sundays. Our parents thought we were at a show in Oakland, like on Broadway Street. The train ride was cool. The train ran on the lower deck of the Oakland–San Francisco Bay Bridge. You could see the ships below, and even get the smell of the water below. It was a great sight. We also could see Alcatraz Prison from the lower deck. The train trip was a short one but exciting.

Once we got off the train we would take an SF Muni streetcar to the ocean side of the city to the big Playland at the Beach. We would head right toward the huge wooden roller coaster, hearing the loud cackling from Laffin' Sal, the wooden lady on her high perch shaking her head every few minutes as she appeared, like a cuckoo clock. The roller coaster was the whole reason for the trip from Oakland to Playland. Usually the air was cold and full with the smell of the ocean. The cool breeze and even the fog were never bothersome. We enjoyed it all the time.

During baseball season we would ride out to Emeryville to Oaks Ball Park and sneak into the game. Baseball was great there, and we had a lot of fun. Oh! The big event was when the carnival and the circus came to town. This was something we all did at night, going on the rides, playing the games, and eating the corn cobs on sticks with lots of butter. The nights were exciting with the vibrant action all around the carnivals. The only problem that did occur was with the older kids age seventeen to twenty. They had grudges against other kids coming out of East Oakland, Jingletown, North Oakland, and some parts of West Oakland. They would fight during some part of the night if they ran into each other.

One big change that Danny and I knew about happened in the late 1940s. The Chinese had a game where you picked numbers and wagered against the house to win large money. I still can remember our regular Chinese man who would come to the door to pick up my mom's numbers. He had a little bamboo brush that he used to mark his copy and your copy. If you wanted, you could go and play your numbers in person.

As a kid I knew a lot of Chinese kids on Seventh and Eighth Streets. They would show us the gambling places in Chinatown. Their people were doing the same thing during the war that all of West Oakland was doing: gambling. It remains a mystery to me how, when I was young, nobody cared, including the police. The police came through the Seventh Street neighborhood all the time. Nobody hid it. They just continued like it was the norm. A lot of people made big money, enough to start small businesses. Like I said, the neighborhood was changing, the cultures of the different people were changing. Even the old-timers, along with the young people born before the war, wanted a different life experience. They wanted to go out to discover new social environments. I believe the start of the 1950s is when people let themselves have fun and not work so hard. The burden of the war let up a little. Fuel was available, and more families had a car that could take them out of the neighborhood. What an experience. And that's the way it was.

My friend Danny and others were experiencing the ups and downs of becoming teenagers when we were in eighth grade. The school at St. Mary's was also going through changes in the late 1940s and early 1950s. In the early 1950s the Fourth of July fireworks were still being displayed at Lake Merritt, with all the Fourth of July activities. Danny and I got into listening to music when we graduated from the eighth grade at St. Mary's. By now we were all moving on to new experiences. Danny was tall and looked older. Somewhere along the way, he bought a 1935 Ford sedan. It ran good. This was about 1952 or 1953. We spent a lot of time keeping the Ford sedan cleaned up and we worked on the engine to make it run smoothly. It was cool to do. We now had wheels to go anywhere in town.

I was working at the Sixth Street Market. Danny had a job at a box factory on High Street. My experience at the Sixth Street Market was valuable to me. I met other kids that worked there who, now that some of us were old enough to get a license and drive, wanted cars. The Sixth Street Market was a unique shopping experience. You had one city block of foods, groceries, and general merchandise, and all varieties of restaurants.

The people who operated their stands in the market, as well as those who worked at the market, were all unique individuals. I got a job working for a Portuguese man, Manuel, who had a large produce stand. He was a very Portuguese-type guy, about five foot eight inches with black wavy hair, dark skin, and a strong body. Maybe with all the produce lifting he developed that muscular look. Manuel had a number one spot in the market, located by the double door going out or in toward the back lot of the building. The market was inside a large steel-frame building. It could have been an old train repair station. It was huge.

The market smelled like chickens; it had a wet smell, the fish, the meat, and barbeque cooking all wrapped in one smell. People were all over shopping, trying to talk the owners down on price.

Today we shop in a peaceful environment with no haggling. In the late 1940s it was fun to shop the Sixth Street Market. If you did not get a lower price, you could shout or smart-talk the owner. They would just tune you out. They were good at keeping people moving on. They never worried about hurting your feelings. That was just how business was done.

My job was to help Manuel bring out the stock from the ice-boxes to keep the stand full for customers. We sold fresh peaches, apples, oranges, potatoes, and anything in season. I had to carry out the lugs of fruits or sacks of potatoes for people. I worked hard. The Saturdays were killers. Going to the market was like going to a Raiders game with crazy people everywhere. The interaction of people was a thing to see and be a part of. The action was upfront and quick. We had about four to five people working the stand along with the owner. Working around the market gave you a lot of interaction with diverse cultures of people and what they expect from the shopping market. My experience of shining shoes at the barbershop helped me learn how people react and behave when out on their own. I am glad I shined shoes before this experience of working at the market.

After working at the fruit stand all day, I got a job cleaning the stand for about ten dollars. I cleaned the produce wooden boxes, stacked them in the back to be shipped back to the farmer's place. Next I would sweep down the stand of all the debris from the produce. Once all the debris was off the wooden stand, I could wash the stand down and scrub wood until the sticky stuff came off. The problem was waiting for the hose. I had to take turns with the other kids who were also cleaning their stands.

The market opened early at 6:00 a.m. and closed about six in the evening. With the multitude of people shoving and push-ing, you could not do any cleaning. All you did was weigh the buyers' produce and take their money. When the market closed, the owners and helpers wanted to go home. They would get us young kids to wash down the stands for a price. One time about four of us kids got together and decided to try to get four to six stands to clean on this Saturday. We would split the money and get out early. We would blitz the stands knowing we would get done before midnight or even earlier. We cleaned fruit stands, fish stands, chicken stands, meat stands. All the guys had to clean: wash and clean the inside glass of the cases; clean, clean, clean. If we did not finish by midnight, the night watchman would lock the doors, set his timer, and not let us out. We would be locked in for the night. So we learned to move fast and work together. We each made about $23 additionally a Saturday. Good money for a kid. This money that we ourselves earned helped us to buy clothing and to have money to go out with our friends, which we did a lot. Now with money, clothing, and the occasional borrowing of a car, we thought we had the world.

Also at this time, music became big with us. The teenager in us came out. We started to go to the local dances. During the late 1940s and early '50s, rock and roll was always our favorite music. Latino music was also moving into jazz, Afro-Caribbean music, and percussion. My brother Mario was a big music fan. He had worked with my dad in the early and middle 1940s in the music shop, so he knew music. When Mario was about eighteen to twenty he had a lot of friends that were musicians or musically talented. These people were as sincere as he was – music was their life.

Dad knew what the bar owners wanted. At this time they liked the cha-cha-cha, Mexican ranchera, bolero, mariachi, and the songs of Agustin Lara. The bar owners usually were people that came from Mexico in the early 1920s and still had their old-country ways. They knew the sadder the song the more beer they sold. During the war, business in the neighborhood bars, restaurants, pool halls, and social clubs kept Seventh Street active. Dad at one point had a few jukeboxes in some of the cafés or bars. Mario and I would do the collections and pay the bar owner the agreed fees, if we had a good day. Mario paid us both off the top before turning in the sack of coins. This would probably be called skimming from your boss. But Dad was not a good payer for this job.

The music I enjoyed was jazz and the Afro-Caribbean, Puerto Rican music. Since Danny was Puerto Rican, we visited many a home and social function. We had friends by now who were into music. We would see them at social functions and dances. Things were changing. Our friends were changing. The neighborhood was going down. People were moving out to the outlying areas of North Oakland, East Oakland, Fremont, and Concord.

When I was real young, I would occasionally go to the show with a kid, Albert Lozano. Albert lived on Castro Street. He had three or four brothers and three sisters. They lived in a two-story Victorian home with a large front porch, typical of that time. One Sunday we decided to go to the show with the older boys. Mike, Albert's older brother, brought along a friend, a percussionist, named Pete Escovedo. They took us up Broadway to the Fox Oakland or the Paramount—I can't remember which—to see a musical. It was my first musical. We usually saw cowboy or space movies at the Rex or Lincoln Theaters, or as we called them, the fleabag theaters. This memory of the musical has stuck with me. I never told Pete that I always remembered that movie trip. The movie theater was nicer inside and the show, *Singin' in the Rain*, was great. It was worth the walk to get there. The Sunday traffic was very light and not like any business day's walk.

Like I said before, times had changed. We now were going to high school and preparing ourselves to start a career. The Sundays became full of social activities: parties, other social events, listening or going to music practice and ballroom dances, if we could get in.

Pete Escovedo and his brother Coke were really into music. Pete is an icon of Latino music in Oakland. I remember following the careers of Pete and Coke. This period of the 1950s was getting very exciting. You had to be on the streets to get the vibes. I had traveled with Danny and some other friends to hear them play at the California Hotel on Sunday afternoons. The Mexican American teens were now into this lively music and jazz. Cal

Tjader, Tito Puente, and Tito Rodriguez, plus many other musicians, made Oakland and San Francisco hot spots. My brother Mario was into the new Latino music. He would spend a lot of time in San Francisco, Oakland, and Berkeley with friends. Mario knew music and had a good ear. At a social event once, he said to me that the Escovedo boys were good and would succeed in this tough business. With Mario's knowledge and experience of these music sounds, I believed his prediction. And he was correct. Not bad for these two West Oakland guys, Pete and Coke, to put this Afro-Caribbean music into our city and all of California.

I still follow Pete's career along with that of his musical family, who I find truly amazing. I get information on the musical family from my nephew and my son, who are musically inclined. Our family is intertwined with the Cheveres. Cecelia Cheveres, the sister of my dear friend Danny Cheveres, married my brother Mario in the 1950s. When Danny and I found out that our brother and sister were going to marry, it was a great time for us. I was very happy to be part of this great family. Unfortunately, Mario and Cecelia divorced. After the divorce, Cecelia became an iconic entertainer in the Bay Area. She was a true Puerto Rican dancer and showgirl.

In the 1950s, Latin percussion music was a powerful influence with young people. The mambo music played by Pérez Prado was hot. This music was percussion played by good musicians. It is easy to dance to, especially with a lot of horns—great stuff. Pérez Prado visited La Ideal Music Shop on Seventh Street. That was an honor.

Danny, myself, and our two or three friends from the neighborhood would hang out all around downtown, at the church with its pool hall basement, and at other people's houses. A kid by the name of Nicolas lived by the railroad tracks about four blocks east of Broadway. The old Victorian house he lived in with his brother and sister was a big place. He had his own place in the basement since he was the oldest son. We would visit him late in the evening to listen to rock and roll music, smoke, and play cards. We all had a great time there with no parents—just the trains rolling by heading to the Mole.

The sound of the train has always been an uplifting experience to me; I find the noise of the train relaxing. We were one block from the Bay and four blocks east of Jack London Square. The square was still depressed then, with most of the wartime joints having closed. The Last Chance Saloon was still there. I remember once when Danny first bought the 1935 Ford sedan, we took a ride from Third and Myrtle Streets to Nicolas's house to break in the sedan. Since the ride passed all the warehouses and foundries, the street was worn down and full of potholes, to say nothing of the Southern Pacific train tracks. It was an interesting ride. We crossed Broadway where you got the smell of food instead of the estuary or bay. Nicolas was home, so we sat on the porch. We talked about many subjects while we were watching the beer warehouse across the street. Men were loading the trucks for the next day's deliveries. When they finished loading a truck they would park it on the sidewalk next to the building, and they would drive another truck inside and repeat the process.

As we watched this over and over, we got an idea. We decided to take some beer cases out of the truck and put them in Nicolas's basement. We did this with no problems. We hit pay dirt. We never took a lot, just enough for ourselves. It was now dark and Danny said, "Let's go to my house." So Danny and I left with some of the beer.

Crossing Broadway heading west, we were stopped by the police. When the cop opened the back door of the sedan, one case of beer fell out onto the cop's foot. *Things are taking a turn for the worse*, I thought. The cop identified both of us. Then he talked with us. He asked us where we got the beer. We told him that we had a bum buy it for us and that we were heading home. In the discussion he asked us what school we were from. We told him St. Mary's, where the priest by that time was Father Gerald Cox. The officer said that he knew Father Cox. "Well, boys," he continued, "here is what we are going to do. You boys tell Father what happened. I will call him to verify this, and if he doesn't know of this incident I will come to your homes and see your parents. I will keep the beer. You boys get on home. And remember, tell the priest the truth." The next day we did tell Father Cox. Father talked with us and we promised him this would not happen again.

At school the next day, Nicolas asked us what happened. He had seen us from his house talking to the cop. We told him the story and that he need not worry, that we told the cop that a bum bought the beer for us in Chinatown, which was three blocks from his house. We told Nicolas that we needed to store the beer at his house and not carry it in the sedan. Nicolas started selling beer out of his basement apartment. The Italian kids would sell you wine out of the barrels of their father's stash in the basement. Most of them had four to six barrels, so who would miss it. Getting liquor in the hands of a teenager was never a problem. Making sure we didn't drink too much was the problem.

Another incident I recall involved the family of one of my St. Mary's classmates. With the shoe shining, selling papers, carrying out at Sixth Street Market, cleaning the stands, and attending school, I was busy. This story involves the family of my classmate and friend, Tony Valdivia. Tony's parents owned El Jalisco Café next to the Star Theater. I remember Tony hanging with us at school. And he would be active in the church's business. Tony, Danny, and myself and others would be in school plays. We had a lot of fun. Tony attended school with us till the eighth grade. Then Tony left to be trained as a Roman Catholic priest for the Archdiocese of San Francisco, which at the time included Oakland.

This incident involves Tony's family, although Tony may not have known this. As with many of us, Tony worked in his family's business, even during grade school. The family owned two eating places. Tony worked at his parents' other restaurant, El Rio Grande on Grove and Seventh Street. Tony's mom was a real people person. She fed the locals and the bracero workers. Her place was a busy one. Tony's dad, I believe, passed on his good looks to Tony. I have a story about me that includes Tony's dad. When I walked home with other kids from our neighborhood after our ballgames, we usually passed Tony's family's restaurant, El Rio Grande. One day we were walking and throwing the baseball back and forth while we walked. I decided on one of the throws that I would hit the baseball with my bat. Well, I did hit it, and I hit it hard. The ball went right through the big plate glass window of El Rio Grande Restaurant. I was going to run like the rest of the boys, but I figured they must have seen me. Besides they knew of my dad's shop down the street. So I stayed and admitted that I did it. Tony's dad with his stocky strong build, just like his son, walked me down to my dad's music shop, where he told my dad what I had just done. Dad agreed to pay Tony's dad, and then I would pay my dad back. Meanwhile Tony was off in the seminary. Maybe he was praying for us.

In 2009, I was able to go to Oakland and see Tony's investiture as a monsignor, an honorary title for a Catholic priest, not bad for a Mexican boy out of West Oakland. When I think back now, in my seventies, I can see what our parents wanted for us, their children, growing up. Our parents worked hard to provide us with a good education by sending us to Catholic schools. Dad came to the USA in 1923 at the age of fifteen. If you saw my notes of Dad's history you would see his work ethic and goals for moving ahead.

THREE

Eye-Openers

———◆◆◆———

A Special Summer

My busy boyhood remained focused on my West Oakland neighborhood. Most of my adventures involved my neighborhood friends, school, and family. The summer of 1948 was an exception and expanded my experience greatly. In this summer my dad and mom drove Mario, Eva, and me to Palaco, Mexico. This town is in Baja California, about thirty miles south of Mexicali. We had relatives there: Uncle Francisco (Pancho), Aunt Tila, and their many children. These relatives were Garcias. They were relatives of my mother, Sara Garcia.

We crossed from Calexico, California, USA, into Mexicali. Mexicali is the capital of Baja California, a state of Mexico. The dirt road to our family's town took us through many a farm area. We saw their fields of cotton, melons, alfalfa, and rows of corn. In arriving in Palaco, most of the houses faced this dirt highway on both sides. All the houses and shops were in adobe buildings. The small adobe houses were square, painted white over the adobe mud.

I recall arriving with our family at my Aunt Tila's house. She had a huge lot and a small house. My Aunt Tila was Mom's oldest sister.

51

They had a special bond. They hugged and kissed each other very warmly. It was easy to see how much they loved each other. We arrived late in the dark. But it was still hot. The ride from Mexicali had been dusty. The road dirt totally covered Dad's old Plymouth.

I was amazed, looking into the house. They were using crystal kerosene lamps with long glass chimneys. I was told they had no electricity, only the kerosene lamps. Mom and Dad slept in the house with the rest of the family. All the boys slept outside under a straw canopy with no lights. Mario and I slept outside in a cot in front of the adobe house. The one thing I noticed was how it was so calm and quiet. The sky was filled with stars, a sight we had never seen in West Oakland. My cousins tried to talk with me in Spanish. I could not understand them. They would laugh and call me *pocho*, meaning a Mexican who was born in the USA.

The morning came with my aunt up early, already sweeping her kitchen floor. This was interesting because the floor was dirt. Because of all the cleaning over time, the dirt was smooth as tile. Aunt Tila asked me to gather wood and put it into the stove so she could begin breakfast. The stove was a wrought iron frame with white porcelain doors. I put wood into it. The kitchen warmed up. It was the only room with heat. The family by now was all up. My cousins helped to fix breakfast with eggs, beans, chorizo, and homemade tortillas.

After breakfast, Mario, a cousin, and I took a walk on the dusty road to Palaco to visit my uncle in his car shop. He lived about a mile away from Aunt Tila. Walking there was dusty, especially when a car came by. The dust rose up and left you dirty with dust! On the way to the shop, we passed a school with a large playing field. The school itself was made of stucco, looking out of place in this small town of adobe buildings. My cousin explained that on Sundays he played soccer on the field and we should come to see him.

When we arrived at the car shop, my uncle was very glad to see us. He had cars, trucks, and farm equipment all around his shop, all needing repair. He told us that he had lived in Oakland in his early years, but he did not like the USA and returned to Mexico. He started this little town called Palaco when he came here with his two sisters, Tila and Enriquetta Garcia. They had made a good life here, and you could see that they were satisfied.

The train stopped in Palaco behind my uncle's shop. This was the event of the day. Uncle lived across the road from his shop. His house might have been larger than his sister Tila's place. It was adobe and his wife kept it clean, even with all the chickens running around. We spent about four hours there, meeting another cousin who only spoke Spanish. In front of the house they had an adobe stand where they sold candy, Chiclets chewing gum, cola, and many *fresca* juice drinks. Palaco was hot so we bought some drinks. I did enjoy the fruit juices. Going back to my aunt's house, we followed the train tracks home. It was hot. We played along the tracks, throwing rocks into the canal that was next to the tracks. My cousin would kneel down and place his ear on the hot track to hear if the train was coming. He had said to Mario and me beforehand that when we got home some of the local kids would be swimming in the canal by the house. We arrived at the swimming hole and we joined the other boys in the water to get relief from the heat. My cousin said that they used this water at home to bathe, to water plants, and for other uses. If we wanted to drink water inside the house, we should drink from the bottled water they had.

On arriving home, the girls were preparing dinner. Some of them were making the tortillas. Watching them prepare the flour, rolling the dough, and hand making the flour tortillas: this was something I had never seen done at home. My sister never took this up. Each night we had beans at dinner and other vegetables, since they grew their own. I now understood why Mom always had beans at dinner for Dad. They were good. One of the interesting drinks we had was tea and lemonade at dinner. *Why tea?* was one of my thoughts.

Mom and Dad had a great visit with Mom's brother and sisters. They told us one night that they would be going back to Mexicali to visit other relatives. Then they would leave for Oakland; Eva was going with them. My dad also wanted to stop in Calexico to do business with an old friend. Dad said Mario and I would go home in a couple of weeks by Greyhound bus, and Mario was in charge. My dad wanted us to know our cousins and the life they lived in Palaco.

These next two weeks were enlightening, exciting, and a playful time. One afternoon my aunt said we could sleep inside since Mom and Dad had left. One of my cousins warned us, "Watch out for scorpions that fall from the straw roof." That night I made the choice to sleep inside. During the night I could not sleep well. Mario slept outside with the boys who were about fifteen years old, the same age as Mario. They all got along good. After that night inside I joined them sleeping outside; I slept much better not thinking about the scorpions falling on me.

Each day we kept busy. First we did the chores early in the morning. We had to bring water from the canal over to the house for cleanup, bathing, and other uses. My aunt with the boys would take two five-gallon cans that were attached by chains to a shoulder bar. The bar fit across your back and was curved for your neck. My aunt with the boys would draw water from the canal, then cross over the tracks and the highway to their adobe house. I would go with the boys to get water but I never had the strength to make it even halfway back. I watched them doing this chore and saw how they were able to do it without much trouble. I would compare that to how easy it was in the city of Oakland to get water out of a faucet and be able to drink it.

As the days moved on, my cousins, male and female, began to enjoy being together. They would kid me about wearing shoes; they stayed barefoot all the time. I tried to go barefoot and it hurt. I don't know how they could step on anything and not be bothered.

Sunday we did go to the soccer events at the stuccoed school's field. My uncle had a team he coached. They sold food, *fresca* juices, and ice cones with fruit flavors. The games and fans would have all the excitement you can imagine. The people came from the local farms, small towns, cattle ranches, and Mexicali. They loved soccer. At night they would have a dance. The school had electricity so we had lights. This event was fun.

Some of the days we had to help my aunt clean the front of her house. It was close to the highway, and the dust would collect on her adobe house and lot. We would rake the front, pick up papers, and rake under the canopy. We kept our sleeping spot clean. Aunt Tila was always cleaning and cooking for all her family and the grandchildren. Like my mother, she was a very clean person. The days were hot. Mario and I helped as much as we could. We teased and played a lot. Our cousins let us join in all their activities. Once our Uncle Francisco took all us kids on his truck down an old road to a watermelon field. He let all the kids get a watermelon. He took a large knife, cut it up, and let us eat our fill. It was great to eat fresh watermelon right out of the field.

On the way back Uncle Francisco told all of us riding in the back of his truck that if we helped him clean his lot and his mechanic's shop, he would take us to San Felipe. San Felipe had a beautiful beach and a weekend was coming. We cleaned up his lot and shop. We left early in the morning in his truck and another car. All totaled, we had six cousins on the trip, plus Uncle Francisco, Aunt Tila, and her husband, Donato. We traveled about thirty miles. The Mexican highway was paved to San Felipe, a tourist location. We arrived early. The homes were built of adobe. The beach was miles long. And the local fishermen had their boats, nets, and docks at the edge of this village. We all had a great time. The beach was clean. The waves were small. We would run out, back and forth, and just had a lot of fun playing. We left in the afternoon to go back to Palaco. Arriving later, we all just crashed in the patio.

Mario and some of the boys his age would go to Mexicali with my uncle to shop for auto parts. I never was invited to go, but Mario said Mexicali was busy with lots of people in the shops. My Aunt Enriquetta did take me shopping with her to Calexico and Mexicali. Her son, my cousin Armando, went also. She took us to a meat market; this was an experience. They had the whole steer hanging in back of a counter. They would cut the piece you wanted right there for you. This open counter arrangement was new to me. I was used to shopping in meat markets in Oakland, such as the Chinese market on Eighth Street where they had all their meats in a refrigerated glass case. The markets on both sides of the border were very busy. People did a lot of shopping, moving across the border. We had no problem crossing either way.

In the last days of our stay, our cousins brought some horses to my aunt's house. These were horses accustomed to being ridden. But I had never ridden a horse before. I thought, *This looks easy to do.* So they put me on a horse alone. I could not understand any instructions they gave me. The horse took off down the road lickety-split. I was scared, yelling at the horse to stop. Lucky for me a man was able to grab the reins. He stopped it and I was very glad. I have never been on a horse since that time.

The summer vacation came to an end. We were driven to Calexico's Greyhound depot to catch the bus to Oakland. On the way back I thought of my cousins and their life in Palaco: the farm work, the dirt highway, adobe houses, sleeping outside, no electricity, the simple life, soccer events on Sunday, the dance, the canal and its water, the bottled water, making tortillas, the scorpions, the trip to San Felipe, the horse ride, meeting so many relatives: what an experience to have had with all that was new to me. I know Dad had a motive for us to learn something from this vacation.

The bus ride back took forever. It seemed to stop in all the Central Valley stations leading to Oakland. When we finally arrived I was glad to be home again. The neighborhood looked great. Mario had been good about taking care of me, and I enjoyed having this time with my older brother. I told Mom that I was glad we lived here in Oakland and that I did not want to live in Palaco, where our people had a hard life. My Aunt Tila, like most of my aunts, died in her late nineties. So I guess the hard work will not kill you. Maybe it's how you are satisfied with your situation that counts.

As an older teenager I did visit Mexico again with Dad and
Mario. We visited relatives and very good friends of Dad's in
Tijuana and Ensenada. I enjoyed Ensenada and Rosarito Beach.
These places were much advanced in catering to the American
tourist. They offered a different experience than I had in Palaco.
Each had its influence on my opinions and thoughts of the country
of my ancestors. As I write this book, Mexico has internal problems that do not encourage visitors. I am glad I saw the Mexico
of my relatives when I did.

A Change of School

Around 1952 Danny and I decided to go to Westlake High on
Grand Avenue. This was a public school, so it was really new to
us. The public school experience was an eye-opener. At this time,
my grade school friends and I seemed to be ahead of the class.
Maybe it was the discipline that we had in the Catholic school.
The Roman Catholic priests plus the Holy Name nuns kept a
tight rein on our behavior. They trained us to pay attention and
respect the ones in charge.

This new experience really changed our social environment. In
the new school we had different classes, different schedules. We
would meet before school, at lunch, and after school. But even at
those times we mixed with everyone else. This school truly was
like a multicultural neighborhood. I use this word only because
it's a big thing now in our country. In my time it was not. We saw
the kids as the Mexican kid, the Jewish kid, the Chinese kid, the
Italian kid, the Irish kid, the Black kid (in those days we said colored kid), and that's the way it was. And it was no big deal. Even
though I attended Westlake Junior School for the first semester
only, I have many memories from it.

All of the students would pretty much keep within their groups,
but not all the time. Sometimes we would mix up, but we knew
each other from West Oakland and St. Mary's. Danny, I believe,
decided to go to McClymonds High School on Twelfth and Market Street because it was closer to his home than Westlake. I know

at Westlake, my friends Ignacio, Nicolas, Manuel, and I were from the same neighborhood. We had other people we knew well, such as the Irish kid, Jim, and his group. In the other groups we knew guys from the ballpark but we never hung out together.

All our friends from the West Oakland neighborhood went there. This school was a long way from Seventh Street. Usually we walked it. We walked from Seventh Street up Broadway to the school. Sometimes we caught the Broadway bus heading north. Mostly we just got there by walking. I knew most of the kids going there from West Oakland, and it was a very multicultural group.

One of the guys I had to go to school with was a boy I had lost a fight to. Now at Westlake High this guy, named Jim, was five foot four and had a solid build. He must have taken the Charles Atlas course. But he was friendly with me. He had a gang of guys he now hung around with from North Oakland. They never bullied anyone. You just kept away from them. Jim's big thing was to maintain control of his group.

Jim and I knew each other from downtown. He lived on Eleventh Street about a half block from Lafayette Square Park, which we called Old Man's Park. When I was about eleven years old, I would go over to his place. It was a single tenant apartment in an old Victorian house. The house had a small porch and a two-door entrance: one for upstairs with the other door for the ground apartment. One day I was over at his place. His parents worked or would be down at the local gin mill, so they were never home. Jim at the time was a very big boy. He used to park his bike on the small porch. When I left his place, three other kids were still in the house. I suppose the bike was on the porch when I left, but I didn't remember seeing it. These kids told him that I took his bike but I never did. Well, that put me into a lousy position. He was out to get me. He came looking for me but I avoided him for months. One thing, Jim was a big Irish kid, very white like a jar of mayonnaise. He had a flat top. I was a skinny Mexican kid that just wanted to get this fight over with. I knew I couldn't beat him.

I talked this over with Danny, and the guys helped me to decide what to do. They had this big thing about honor, respect, dignity, and cowardice. So one of them would talk to Jim, and we would meet at Old Man's Park at a given time to do whatever. Jim was right to be upset. The crime of stealing your bike at that time was like stealing your horse in the 1850s, as in the movies we saw at the Rex Theater. They hang you. Old Man's Park was a city block where the old men drank, gambled, played checkers and dominoes, and argued all day long. This place always had a smell like old alcohol or wet pee on clothing. This park was blocks from city hall. The day came, and I showed up with my four friends. Jim had his four or five friends. We fought. I lost. But they never bothered me after that. They actually helped me in a few tight spots later, as we grew older. Who took the bike was of no concern. I showed up. Jim was happy. He won, and he kept his reputation with all the kids. The high school crowd knew who was in charge. I have seen Jim in later years. He was a man who still had his old four cronies with him.

Another big episode that happened at Westlake was a controversy between two guys that got out of hand. What happened was an African American kid (I don't know his name) called out a Filipino kid whose name was Francisco. Francisco lived in North Oakland around Nineteenth or Twentieth Street. I knew of him and had seen him a lot on Seventh Street. He had a couple of brothers that hung out on Seventh Street, at the pool hall with the older guys. They were sharp dressers, as I remember, because the older guys dressed sharp, always looking clean and neat, doing their thing. The controversy was that Francisco did not back down but took this guy on. Francisco beat the kid up real bad. Francisco was five foot five inches and was built like a tank. And he knew martial arts.

The next day the African American kid told Francisco that his friends wanted a new fight. Francisco told him, "Good. My brothers will be here also." The school had gangs from Oakland neighborhoods all across the city, including West Berkeley and Richmond with a mix of kids that were African American, Mexican, Irish, Filipino, and many others.

Francisco was like my friend Ignacio. They both thought things out. Neither wanted any part of a fight. Their plan was always to get this over with now. With his brothers behind him, Francisco knew that he would have a lot of support. This was true. The fight happened again and Francisco won. The message was sent: Don't mess with us again, not in school and not on the streets.

This was my first experience with gangs that would not back down on any confrontation or controversies. Like I said, things were changing all over Oakland. The old-timers could see that the youth were going to be more adventurous in searching out new places and areas for hanging out. The old traditional ways of mutual respect and staying in the neighborhood were fading. I had not recognized the loyalty that the gangs demanded until this fight happened. I knew these gang members as individuals and friends. And I knew many of them from both sides. But each group lived in a different neighborhood and the cultures reacted with instincts of surviving. After the fight everybody settled down and went back to getting along.

One thing different from today is how kids fought. In our time you fought person to person with your fists or with other body skills like martial arts. You knew who you were fighting and why. You looked each other in the eye, whether you thought you would win or not. And your friends had your back. No dirty tricks. No sneaking up from behind with a knife. No using a gun from a safe distance. And after the fight was over, it was over. This is something else that has changed. Our way of dealing with each other included negotiation. Today's kids need to develop their ability to deal with conflict without killing each other.

At this time, one of our good friends who lived on Myrtle Street moved to Little Italy in North Oakland. We had known Gino since Tompkins Elementary School. In 1942 he lived next door to Danny. Gino was a tall, stocky kid with dark black curly hair who had a five o'clock shadow on his face. Gino's house always had food. His mom would feed us Italian sausage with red and green peppers and sourdough bread produced in Oakland. I will always remember the sandwiches his mom fixed us and how well we were treated. Gino, like all the kids in the neighborhood, never had any money, since his dad was a laborer. His dad drove an old black Dodge pickup truck with wooden sides. The Dodge pickup had a unique sound. All Dodges did. You could tell a Dodge from a Ford by its sound.

Gino had two younger brothers whose names I don't remember right now. We would ride up to Fortieth or Fiftieth Street to visit Gino. He would take us around the area. It was a nice old neighborhood with businesses on Telegraph Avenue: Italian delicatessens, markets, and restaurants. Bertola's on Forty-Fifth Street at the intersection of Shattuck and Telegraph was a great place for family-style meals. During this time I never ate there, but in the 1960s I would eat there with my wife and family. Also in this area was a well-known candy company, Hooper's Chocolates, on Telegraph Avenue. Gino would take us to swim at the city pool behind Oakland Technical High School. I don't remember paying anything to get in. Gino had a new set of friends we met and got along with.

However, we lost track of Gino as time passed, and as other things around us were changing. I did meet Gino once in 1955 at the Colombo Club in his neighborhood. Other old friends, like Gino, were moving out of the area. Back in the neighborhood we felt our loss of these old friends. The area had taken on a depressed look. Businesses, light manufacturing businesses especially, were moving out of the area.

Change All Around

As the 1960s approached, change continued. People wanted to experience change. Pot was more out in the open and easier to get. Most people could buy it in many locations. On Seventh Street, the Mexican youth had experience with this product in the early

1940s in the pachuco era. Many people paid no attention to what was going on, as long as nothing was disturbing their lives. Most of the kids born in the 1930s were ignoring their parents' old-country ways. The church in many ways was trying to replace the parents' responsibility of trying to keep the kids away from gangs and drugs. Anyone could get pot if they wanted it and searched around a little. Nobody was pushing people to get it. Today in the early twenty-first century, I can't believe how emotions of the public can react so strongly against this product. Pot has been around a long time. It is not going away.

I can remember people driving in fancy cars into the Seventh Street area in the late 1940s and 1950s to buy pot. Since I worked in my dad's shop, I was not surprised to see the fancy cars at the creamery or the pool hall across from the music shop. I once asked Mario what was going on. He said the gringo was waking up to this new experience, especially the young people. We talked about pot. He spoke of old families that had a hand in getting pot into the Seventh Street scene. He said that the gringos from Orinda and Moraga would take it into Berkeley to sell at the college. Seventh Street from Adeline Street on the west to Broadway on the east was occupied by Mexican or Latino people during this time, and most people knew the local gangs had business going on with pot.

This period saw the expansion of people moving out to other areas of Oakland and the suburbs. I was still working at the Sixth Street Market and helping to clean the stands at night. I met an old friend named Ignacio who happened to live on Myrtle Street. He had older brothers and three younger sisters. Ignacio and I became friends again, and about this time I introduced him to Danny. Since he lived just a few blocks away, we all spent a lot of time together. Ignacio was my height, about five feet and seven inches. He was a very strong stocky guy with a dark complexion and wavy black hair. Ignacio was a thinker. He always had a way of advising Danny and me about being cool with certain people that we met. Ignacio's brothers were into activities that we kept away from. Even Ignacio would tell us to keep away from them. They had a thing going in the neighborhood that produced money for them and could not be discussed.

When I transferred from Westlake High School to St. Elizabeth High School after the first semester of my freshman year, I no longer saw some of my best friends on a day-to-day basis. As good as my job at the Sixth Street Market was, it didn't take up all my time. So Danny and our friends would hang out at each other's houses. At night Andy's Drive-In on Grand Avenue was a great place to meet up with kids. The burgers were cheap and the milk shakes were good. We visited this place a lot. We knew lots of people there.

When we wanted a really good hamburger, I liked Gus the Greek's Burgers at Seventh Street and Franklin, in Chinatown. This hole in the wall was truly the hamburger palace. And it had a pinball machine. Another place we patronized was a small round white building on First Avenue by the lake. It was called Casper's Famous Hot Dogs. This place started in Oakland in 1934. What a good time to open a business. They are still in town. These people were Armenians. Immigrants understood the hot dog and the hot dog customers. Their hard work and fresh food made this hot dog the best. They had a special bun, and the wiener was a special sausage. These hog dogs had all the trimmings. When you said, "Let's get a hot dog," only Casper's came to mind. There used to be a Doggie Diner in Oakland that tried to take over the hot dog market but never did. They never had a hot dog with the consistent quality of Casper's.

During this time Danny and I would go all over the city. The 1950s was a great time. Oakland as a city had activities going on all the time. The Oakland Auditorium would put on auto shows, sporting events, circuses, boxing and wrestling matches, midget car races, cultural events, and big band dances. We all would get together and go somewhere, like the Oakland Speedway, to have a good time. This speedway was on East Fourteenth Street and 150th Avenue in San Leandro near the Drug King drugstore, at

Bay Fair Shopping Center (now Bayfair Center). The Oakland Speedway was for stock cars. It closed down in 1954. Another popular place was a midget racetrack in the Exposition Building. This oval track was one-twelfth mile, or about 440 feet around. These midget cars made lots of noise and spewed lots of fumes. It was really something to see and lots of fun. We also went to Oakland's Grand National Roadster Show until 1998, when it began to be held in various locations.

Danny and I with a few friends would also go over to San Francisco in the 1935 four-door sedan. When we were around fifteen to seventeen years old, we went over to the big dance hall in San Francisco. It was a large white building on a hill next to a 76 gas station. They had Latino dances there. Growing up and in grade school we spent our time in the neighborhood. Then as teenagers we were always going somewhere to make sure we didn't miss anything. When Danny and I attended different schools, we lost contact. Then his mom moved out to East Oakland close to MacArthur Boulevard.

At that time I had a job at Leo Baum's Normal Pharmacy. I would deliver prescriptions to people's homes on my bike. Leo had his store on Tenth and Broadway across from my newsstand. I believe that is how I got the delivery job. My route was from Tenth and Broadway to the second store up Broadway to Pill Hill. A guy named Mush ran that store. He was a tall man, about six foot one with a heavy body and a strong voice. The store delivered east of Tenth and Broadway to Alice Street and west to Market Street. This job was okay for me on the bike while I attended St. Elizabeth High School in East Oakland.

Leo also had two Chinese guys driving a green panel truck that delivered all over the town. These fellows sold fireworks in Chinatown for the Fourth of July. Leo was a sharp businessman who always was friendly. He knew how to greet people with a sincere smile and good handshake. He knew his clients. If the bike deliveries were slow I would go with the drivers to make a delivery. We stopped at the city hall sometimes, and went up Broadway to Piedmont, then along Lake Merritt for special customers. Leo liked the politics of Oakland's city hall and downtown. I still lived at 724 Seventh Street. You could see that businesses on Seventh Street were slowly closing down.

By this time I missed the streetcars we had when I was a child. Around 1948 they had eliminated these streetcars and replaced them with buses. It was never the same. We also heard rumors then of the new freeway coming through West Oakland and that the new Chevy plant was going to Fremont. Other businesses connected to the auto industry were also moving out of Oakland. Somewhere during this time in high school, I would see my old friends Danny, Ignacio, Nicolas, Manuel, and Francisco. They were all changing. Maybe we just were growing up and the neighborhood in West Oakland had its last fight to survive.

High school in the 1950s at St. Elizabeth was a great experience. The school had a great mix of kids. The kids never seemed to have any problems interacting together . . . all of them. I started going with Anita Garcia in 1954. She was very attractive and a lot of fun. I met her through my brother, who was a couple of grades, I believe, ahead of her. And she was one school year ahead of me. When I decided to go to St. Elizabeth High School, he told me about her and I did search her out. The first time I saw her in study class, I knew that was it. I knew a lot of girls but I was never into going with any one girl in any serious way. I just got along with them well and had respect for them. Once Anita and I hit it off, we did stick together. It was my best and only decision, that I knew we would stick together forever.

By now I was learning that St. Elizabeth High School had its standards just like St. Mary's School. The Franciscan priests with their brown robes and ropelike sashes were as strict as the Roman Catholic priests were at St. Mary's. East Oakland was a much cleaner neighborhood than Seventh Street. The local houses around the school were kept up and families lived in them.

I had met new friends by now and we hung out all through East Oakland, mostly by the Fruitvale Theater and a place for hot dogs, burgers, and pinball machines. I was new to East Oakland so meeting Salvador and Marcus was good. They knew East Oakland and the guys and girls that hung out here. We spent lots of quarters on the pinball machines. It was a serious game when you played. The trick was to get free games on the counter that tracked the games. Some people would play and constantly win free games for the pinball machines. I would say they were like kids who today would spend all their time texting.

Salvador lived on Thirty-Eighth Avenue, a few blocks north of MacArthur Boulevard. I spent a lot of time with Salvador. By now I had bought a car, and he knew how to repair it, which was a big help to me. Your own car is a big thing to a junior in high school. I had also gotten a job at Lilly Pharmacy on Pill Hill. A friend of mine, Freddie, was going to work at Red's Tamales, a tamale factory in East Oakland. He asked me if I wanted this job. I said sure. The bike job at Leo's was getting to me because of the outside elements and traffic. I took my bike up to Frenchie's Bike Repair on San Pablo Avenue. I knew Frenchie when he was much younger. He was now an old man with a leather apron and a cap that he wore all the time. He always had bifocal glasses on his nose. He looked like Geppetto in the Disney movie *Pinocchio*. The old building inside had a wood floor, tool benches, vises, and bikes all over. Since Frenchie knew me and had put most of the parts onto my bike to give it comfort and speed, he gave me a fair price in cash.

The new job was on Pill Hill at Twenty-Ninth and Summit, down the street from Providence Hospital. Lilly had two pharmacies, both on Twenty-Ninth Street across from each other. My job was to make deliveries to the doctor's offices and keep the pharmacy clean. This job was a learning experience for me plus it helped me on expenses for three years of high school. I worked with Palmer, a pharmacist. He taught me a lot. I learned how to make all types of suppositories, tooth powders, and an elixir in four-ounce bottles for all kinds of ailments. As my years there moved along, Palmer let me do more. We got to know each other well. He was about five foot four, a slender man with white hair and with an eye for style, for he was a sharp dresser and a real gentleman.

Palmer taught me how to answer the phones. We had about twenty doctors in the building with lines coming directly to the pharmacy. When he would get busy, he would let me answer the phones. The doctors gave me the prescription on the phone, or the head nurse did. I also ran the register, made ointments, salves, filled bottles of cold elixirs – anything to help him. Palmer taught me much about the pharmacy business. He placed a lot of trust in me. I felt confident in doing my job. Today they have aides in the big pharmacies. I was doing this in the early 1950s. Palmer lived in Alamo and would drive into Pill Hill every day in an old Nash car, long and sleek. He would buy me lunch once in a while, if I would drive to George's Café on Telegraph Avenue to get one of their hamburgers with fries. This place made a long hamburger six inches across and three-quarters of an inch thick on a French bun. Palmer could not eat it all. I would get half. It was a good Saturday on the hill on hamburger day.

Mr. Lilly worked in the main store that was larger, with more doctors, at the Summit Avenue location. Here they had two more pharmacists. Mr. Lilly was a partner with an Italian man named Basil Panella. Mr. Lilly was a German Jewish man, short and chunky with white hair. He also was a fancy dresser. He liked to drink and was single. He lived in a very nice apartment on Grand Avenue. Mr. Lilly would let me use his Oldsmobile Rocket to make special deliveries to his friends. Palmer said he liked to hang out at Trader Vic's on Telegraph Avenue. Basil was a father raising two boys, one girl, and supporting his father. He lived off MacArthur Boulevard. Basil was the dad of one of my Italian friends. He was five foot eight and always had a five o'clock shadow. Basil was very frugal and devoted to his children, a very good man. He always liked me, I know, because he showed me a lot of respect and kidded me a lot.

Near the end of my high school years I met Ignacio one night at the Doggie Diner on Fruitvale and East Fourteenth Street. He surprised me with news that Danny had quit school and was joining the Air Force. I realized that I had drifted away from Danny after we got more involved with our different high school friends. It was good to see Ignacio, my old friend that I had grown up with. Ignacio was now living on Twenty-Third Ave in Jingletown with his mom. He had just finished high school and was working. I did see him once in a while on East Fourteenth Street but now we all had split up and had different friends and social activities.

This was a time for weddings, for us and for many of our friends. Anita graduated a year ahead of me. I married Anita on March 17, 1956. We had a big wedding at a local church, and the wedding reception was held in a nice hall. All our families attended. We had great music. The wedding was a big event in this family. As soon as I married Anita, I was accepted into her large Puerto Rican and Portuguese family. For them, Anita was a favorite niece and cousin. I knew she was special. She had the respect of the family members.

Today, after celebrating over fifty-five years of marriage, it's like we just got started. We talk about issues and resolve them and move forward. We don't dwell on them; just move forward with a positive commitment. That's the best advice I would give anybody, if you are sincere on making it work.

Before I graduated from high school, Basil and Mr. Lilly asked me if I wanted to be a pharmacist. They would help me financially, and I would pay them back by working with them. I declined the offer, and I regret that I did. Now I wish I had had a mentor's guidance in making this decision. In hindsight I think it would have been a good learning experience. I now think all young people should have someone to mentor them in the growing-up periods of life. Wouldn't that help all the kids? Some of us just need that kind of help.

We had an African American guy, Joe, working with us. Joe and I got along well. I would give him a ride home at night and on certain days I would pick him up for work. Joe lived with his parents on Seventy-Ninth or Eightieth Avenue. He was short with a stocky build. He loved to talk and had a good outlook on life. Later I did see Joe on East Fourteenth Street at different times.

In West Oakland you couldn't miss the continuing changes. People had moved out; the old Victorian houses were being torn down for the post office and the coming freeways. Dad's La Ideal Music Shop had lost its customer base. Mario now had a job with Chatton Distributors, which handled records, on Grove Street. I was finishing high school and working at Lilly Pharmacy. Like I said, things were changing. Seventh Street lost its business base. Latino people were moving all over, not just to Fruitvale Avenue. The car plant moved to Fremont, and the foundries moved. Also Southern Pacific had changed. The Mole was slowing way down, and downtown was dying. No people, no shoppers; the outlying centers were becoming Fremont, Walnut Creek, Concord, Pleasant Hills, Pinole. Oakland was at a loss. In 1956 I graduated from St. Elizabeth High School. After this period I lost track of many of my friends. My dear friend Danny was in the service. The war in Korea was reaching a truce so the draft slowed down.

I was still working on Pill Hill when I decided to go to Moler Barber College on Tenth and Broadway to be a barber. The course was six months. Then you had to pass the state board exam for your apprentice license. During this time, 1956 and 1957, I also worked at the Fruitvale Cannery during the summer season. I must have been nineteen years old. I would go to school 8 a.m. to 3 p.m. Then I would go to work at the cannery until 11 p.m. or midnight, go home, sleep, and be back at school by 8 a.m. This school was Monday through Friday. By now all my friends were doing their thing. Some moved on to college. Some had jobs. A few just hung out in the neighborhood. We still had some of the small mom-and-pop stores open, as well as the cleaners, the small grocery stores, the Star Theater, the creamery, and the pool hall. The small shops survived because most of them were family-owned and all the family worked the business. I would help my dad in the music shop and practice haircuts to help me in school.

One of our friends, Ignacio, still hung out on Myrtle Street below Fourth Street. He would come by the shop and talk with me. We both were about twenty then. I was working and going to school. Ignacio was still searching for his career. I would lend him my sport coats so he could attend the dances. I would kid him, saying that if he ever got into a fight to please take the jacket off. Ignacio and I had known each other since Tompkins Elementary School. He had two brothers that still were involved in the neighborhood and had expanded their business to Berkeley, North Oakland, Piedmont, and Hayward. Ignacio had said he would help them at times but they were hard to deal with and it wasn't for him. He knew that he had to get out of the neighborhood.

By 1957 you could see that the atmosphere in Oakland was declining. In fact, in West Oakland it was plain bad. People had many issues. The people felt left out of city hall decisions. Even learning about major changes in the city or plans in our neighborhood was difficult. City staff didn't answer questions. You could see that all the different cultures in our twelve square blocks were beginning to relocate to the suburbs and other areas of Oakland. We had no stability in West Oakland. The city officials never sent out a clear message of what had happened or what they were doing. The worried old-timers, the people left behind, and the youth in any of these races or cultures had no faith in the changes the city officials wanted. West Oakland had lost its neighborhood pride by the late 1950s. The coming unrest through the 1960s to the 1970s would be like a long foggy day moving all through Oakland to its borders.

FOUR

Early Jobs and Family

————◆◈◈◆————

After graduation, barber school and work kept me, a young father, very busy. This period of the late 1950s was a trying time. I finished the barber school and passed the state board exam the first time. Now I had to go out and find a job to make some money. My brother Mario was still working for Bob Chatton. Mario had married Cecelia Cheveres, Danny's sister, and they had a baby boy, Mario Jr. They had moved to Fortieth and Grove Street in North Oakland. The building they lived in looked like two duplexes stacked on top of each other. It was a nice place. Anita and I would visit them at times to see the new baby.

My mom and dad were happy to be grandparents. They were very happy that Mario had married Cecelia Cheveres. Cecelia's mom, Isabel, and Antonio, her dad, were special people. I loved them as I did my own mom and dad. My friend Danny and I were happy for ourselves. He liked Mario, and I loved the Cheveres family.

I believe my first job as a barber was at the Key Barber Shop at the Key Card Room and Café. It was a two-chair shop right next to the Key Hotel on San Pablo Avenue. The shop had a shoeshine stand, manicurist, and two barbers. Even with all this activity it was a clean shop. The shop had a customer base of people that were gamblers next door in the card room. The real pros would come in late afternoon to get a trim shave, manicure, or a shine, getting ready to gamble at the tables. In the hotel upstairs they had a room for the big players with big money, not the locals who would gamble at the table with the rest of the people. The games upstairs were for special people.

In my training at the Moler Barber College, they taught us each to shave customers with a straight razor. It's one of the hardest things to learn. I did learn how to use the straight razor and in this Key Barber Shop I gained a lot of practice. It helped me with the clients the shop had. As time went on I gained customers. The owner of the Key Card Club was an old guy that wanted a hair trim, shave, shoeshine, and manicure daily. So he put a shop into the Key Hotel. This guy had an old friend with him all of the time. He was a Mexican by the name of Tiny. This name fit him. Tiny was the owner of the Tiny Drive-In on Grand Avenue and Harrison. This was one of the drive-ins we kids went to. It was a busy place in Oakland. Both the Key Card Club owner and Tiny were what I would call a couple of old characters, and very interesting. They dressed in classy suits and looked very dapper.

Doc, the owner of the Key Barber Shop, was an English man, thin, about five foot eight with white balding hair. We all worked with Doc in the shop. It was a good place to get more training for me to get my journeyman license. Emeryville was across MacArthur Boulevard in Oakland. The shop was south of the old Oaks Ball Park, which I remember well. I must have worked at this shop for about a year.

I moved on from the Key Barber Shop to a shop at the Tribune Tower. They had a nice shop on the ground floor. George was the owner. He was a tall barber about five foot nine, rosy cheeks, with a very light complexion. The shop was a busy barbershop. It was in a good location in the downtown business section. From this shop I moved to San Lorenzo, to the Larson Barber Shop. A friend of mine, Johnny Sanchez, worked here. I had gone to barber school with him. I bounced around a lot. Barbering at this time was not paying much. Weekly, it was hard. Johnny was going with Vangie, who was one of Anita's friends and my school friend. They married in the 1950s.

I would occasionally see some old West Oakland friends and some of the kids I grew up with. Since downtown was still active in the late 1950s and early 1960s, it was easy to bump into them. Almost all of them still lived in lower West Oakland, past Market Street heading west to the Mole. They had made changes in their lives like I did, but still lived on Myrtle Street or close by. They told me most of the old people were moving out to Fruitvale, East Oakland, North Oakland, or Hayward. The kids wanted out of West Oakland.

The old neighborhood had no appeal for people of my generation. They wanted the new homes in areas that had good schools without all of the issues that West Oakland had in the early 1960s. The 1960s brought out a lot of people that wanted change. This was true for both the African American and Mexican people still in the neighborhoods. In the early 1960s through 1966, the Black Panthers came on the scene. Led by Huey Newton, they developed social programs in West Oakland and had social agendas. They were part of the scene in the neighborhood on Market Street. They also had it in for the Oakland police because of the brutality that the police department had shown to the Black man. I told my friends to remember what our older brothers had said of the Oakland police and their treatment of West Oakland Mexican people, especially the pachucos in the 1940s. From the early 1930s to the 1950s, there was cause to make an issue of the brutal treatment of the Mexicans and others from that region. I also told my friends now hanging out in East Oakland that we knew a couple of people that had joined a new bike club on Foothill Boulevard. One of the guys was Ralph "Sonny" Barger. His club was the Oakland Chapter of the Hell's Angels. So, yes, we were seeing a lot of changes in the late 1950s and into the 1960s in Oakland.

I met the Garcias in the early 1950s. (These Garcias are not related to Anita's family.) The Garcia boys, Art and Stanley, were well-known in East Oakland and throughout the Bay Area. They had a couple of sisters who would come on Saturdays to La Ideal Music Shop. My brother, Mario, would entertain them with the new recordings. They were attractive girls and the shop was buzzing while they were there. Mario always had different groups come by on Saturdays to see him.

I would visit my dad's shop, La Ideal, in the early 1960s when I was still barbering in the shops. I would enjoy the old-timers that would stop at the shop with their political opinions on the history of our area and of the Mexican American relations. Now that I was about twenty-three, I could question them on the subject; as a boy I just listened. They would talk of *La Leyenda Negra* or "The Black Legend." This was the negative view of Hispanic societies that goes back to the 15th century when Spain conquered so much land in the New World, and other countries were jealous. The English and Dutch were enemies of Spain and considered themselves the superior race. This hate came down to the people of Latino ancestry being talked down and considered untrustworthy. The cruelty of the conquistadors did not help. This image of Spanish people as a cruel, loose, greedy, lazy, noisy, slick race was the propaganda being spread and written by the English and Dutch that hated the Spaniards' success.

This viewpoint was known as the "Black Legend." This invisible hate started by the idea of the superior white man is still present today. The discussion in the barbershop would bring up many discrimination issues going back to the early Californios and Mexicans. In Oakland during the 1920s through the 1940s, Mexicans were limited by local restrictions. Mexicans could not live or buy a house in certain areas of Oakland. This discrimination did not help the ongoing discussion and conflict of *La Leyenda Negra*. This Anglo attitude towards Mexican Americans was something that the young people my age talked about. The Black Legend is something that we can say continues even today, in the beginning of the twenty-first century.

I still see the stories of immigration issues that blame Mexican or Latino immigrants for additional expenses in state budgets. The expenses of illegal or undocumented immigrants have varying causes. They cannot be blamed on Mexican immigrants. The media has brought up the discrimination topic with articles in this twenty-first century. The illegal immigration issue never seems to go away, just like discrimination against the African Americans never goes away. In both cases most Latinos and African Americans are descended from ancestors who arrived in America long before the ancestors of many so-called American patriots.

I once asked my dad and my mom why and how they came to Oakland in the early 1920s. Was the border crossing a big deal to them? They knew of the old stories when all this land where we live was Spanish and then Mexican land (and the land of the ever-forgotten Indians). The border in 1920, my dad said, was like a good Sunday walk. He had received all his legal paperwork at the immigration border office and came across in the 1920s to work. The opportunity was much better in the USA than in his small pueblo so he came over to live the better life. Mexico at that time was a failed state.

The 1910 Revolutionary War had left Mexico broke. Dad said the war had been devastating for the people at the lower level. My mom said to me that her family was from Parral, Chihuahua, *Tierra de Guerra*—Land of War. Her parents worked for General Pancho Villa. My grandfather was a farmer and worked the Pancho Villa lands, sometimes as a sharecropper. My grandmother was the cook for the Pancho Villa family. Mom was very proud of her family bloodline. She was Mexican, French, and Spanish. I myself have not checked this out, but my cousin claims we could also have Moorish blood in us. When I look back on our history as a family, I know we were multicultural. When different cultures today try to tie their life to their people who lived before them, they need to respect the history. The important thing is we are here and they are gone. We need to keep exploring where we came from because as a Mexican American and first-generation American, I have a mestizo background, and I am a human being.

I respect this heritage of mine and remain open to learning any other information.

As I said, my dad and mom walked across the border after getting their paperwork from the border officials. Our American government has been neglectful for a long time in securing the border. Until our president and the Congress take the documentation issue seriously and make the border not only secure but also appropriate for legal immigration, we will have no control on who comes into America. This is not like the 1920s. The legal entry must be part of the new changes in our daily lives. The people crossing must be legal and follow the current laws of our immigration processes. Why cannot a person show his legal papers to be here to the border officials? These papers can then be acknowledged at job sites, hospitals, and all the public assistance places.

I also believe what Mom and Dad would tell us at home: "You learn English and learn it well enough to educate yourself to get ahead in the country to have a better life."

On one of my visits to Dad's La Ideal Music Shop, I ran into Freddie Juarez. Freddie happened to be the kid that got me the job with Bill Lilly and Basil Panella in Pill Hill. It was good to see Freddie. He was still with Red's Tamales. I asked Freddie about his brother, Tommy Juarez. Tommy, like Tony in the eighth grade, had left to be a priest. Freddie said that Tommy, now a Salesian priest, was doing well and good. He was still in the priesthood in San Francisco. Freddie and his parents lived on Sixth and Adeline Street.

I did not have much time to hang out with my old school and growing-up friends. I would see them once in a while on East Fourteenth Street. We would talk about old times in the neighborhood. Some of them were going on to college and planning stable careers, like their immigrant parents wanted them to do. A few of them chose a different path. I know that if they had had the guidance, they could have avoided a life of criminal activities. You have to remember we lived in a workingman's neighborhood where certain activities were considered normal. One of them was gambling. It was normal that most people gambled at the pool hall and other places of gambling such as card rooms in the back of a bar or café, or at a social hall, or church halls, and who knows but for some, even dice on the streets. I always did well throwing a quarter against a wall. It was a normal thing to do. Some of the kids could do well in gambling. They never gave it up. They just expanded it to a bigger game. These types of people enjoy this life of chance and being around the excitement of winning. Today it's playing bingo or visiting Thunder Valley or another Indian casino.

Like I said, all my friends had changed. I was lucky. My parents had always been home after school. Some of the kids had both parents working when they grew up. They had jobs at the shipyard and at that time many a latchkey kid was on his own at a young age. The Second World War, I believe, had changed the culture of so many of us first-generation kids. We saw a lot: people changed; they worked hard, so they played hard. The times for all the people had changed. It was an exciting time with lots of things going on. We were near the ships at port and the bases all around. If you were lucky that no one in your family was killed or badly injured during the war, as a kid you were ready for adventure.

When Danny Cheveres got out of the service, he returned to Oakland. He had been now out of the service a couple of years. I had not seen him since he was out. Danny was married now. We went to their home to visit. He lived across from the Del Monte cannery on Fruitvale Avenue next to the freeway and the railroad track. The smell of the tomatoes from the cannery hid the smell of the diesel trucks and trains zooming by. This street would take you to Twenty-Third Avenue or Jingletown. It was good to have him back. Danny was a true friend. He was loyal, respectable, honest, and honorable. I trusted Danny, and I had had a good relationship with him since Tompkins Elementary School in West Oakland. When my brother Mario married Ceci, I became part of

Danny's family – a Cheveres relative. I remember when we were about seventeen years old, Danny would get me to go with him to the home of Eva (his future wife) in Emeryville. I would go in the 1935 Ford sedan so Danny could visit with her. My job was to watch the car. She lived in an area worse than ours. When my first son, Steve, was born, Danny was my choice as the godfather. As the years passed by we had more kids. I baptized Danny's kid, little Danny Junior. Life had really changed us.

I left barbering after working in San Lorenzo at Larson's Haircuts and got a full-time job with one of Oakland's major drugstore companies, PayLess. I would still visit the old neighborhood and help my dad in the barbershop and record shop. The old-timers would still come by, talk, have a drink of old Mexico whiskey, and gamble a bit. Seventh Street now was dying. Most of the old stores, the butcher shop, Lozano's Shoe Repair, cleaners, cafés, bars, and others were closing up. Many of my friends were now hanging out downtown at Thirteenth and Broadway. They also had changed. When businesses started closing in the early 1960s, West Oakland lost its luster. Seventh Street no longer was a safe street. New people coming in had killed the sense of safety in all areas. You could feel the change. Working in my new job, I applied myself to learning all I could. The company policy was to promote from within. You did not have to be a graduate of a college to move ahead.

I started at PayLess in 1958. They put me on the graveyard crew for at least two or three years. I learned a lot about stocking inventory, the company, retail, and the people in the company. I believe we had three or four stores at the time: Oakland, San Jose, Stockton, and Sacramento. My boss at night was a hard worker and knew his job well. In the 1960s the drugstore was a big volume business, and the Oakland store did the big business. We controlled the drugstore business. Our Oakland store was at 1901 Telegraph Avenue across from Capwell's.

Anita and I were very young at the time. We might have been living with her mom or dad. For a while we also lived in a small cottage behind Rosie Adelman's house in East Oakland. I know we had our first son, Stevie, with us. The place had a small front room, small kitchen, and small bedroom. We had a lot of fun there. The place was a busy one. Rosie had an old father living with her. He was about eighty or ninety years old. He lived in the basement of Rosie's house. Our place was in the backyard of Rosie's house. We had an outside patio between us. Sometimes the old man would just come into our house and then walk out. One time he left the house and they found him in San Francisco. He got around; that was why you had to really watch him. Rosie also had a brother, Frankie. He was slow but he was good to us. Frankie was a big guy about six feet tall, 290 pounds. Although he was mentally slow, he was able to hold a job. He worked at the Palmolive factory in Emeryville. Rosie had a lot of people coming and going from her house. We never lacked any activity around us. In this time we had very little money for anything extra. Anita's parents, Mae and Bill, always had company in their house on Eighty-Ninth Avenue. The aunts and uncles were always around. Also most of them lived in East Oakland, Jingle-town, Twenty-Third Avenue, East Twelfth Street, and around East Oakland. Anita's Uncle Wally and Aunt Minnie lived on Seventy-Ninth near the Chevy plant.

Anita's family gave us lots of things to do. When the family was going fishing, hunting, or to a party (and they had many activities like these), Anita was always welcome. As I met more of her family, I realized I had met her cousin, Norman Rivera, in East Oakland when I was in high school at the hamburger joint by the Fruitvale Theater. He hung around a rough crowd. I knew most of the guys, and I never hung out with them. But we all associated, and I knew a lot of people. The place for us was the Fruitvale Theater and the hamburger joint. You learn, like I said, from your growing up knowing a lot of kids. You learn how to avoid conflict with any one person or group by attending only to your business. They get to know you, and they leave you alone. The stranger interfering with the group will get hurt. Respect is a big thing.

Tony Lema, the pro golfer, was also from Oakland. He was born February 25th, 1934, and died July 24, 1966, in an airplane crash in Chicago. Tony grew up in a largely industrial neighborhood on the border between East Oakland and San Leandro. He was just three when his dad died in 1937. His dad was of Portuguese descent. He had attended St. Elizabeth High School in East Oakland. He was in my brother Mario's class. Tony was always the charmer, full of mischief but not a delinquent. He did get into trouble with the police sometimes with his mischievous pranks. Tony caddied at age twelve at Lake Chabot Golf Course in the Oakland Hills for coach Lucius Bateman, an African American man. By age thirteen Tony was playing under the guidance of Dick Fry. At age eighteen he won the Oakland City Amateur Championship. He met John Brodie, also another young golfer. At this time they were roommates on the tour. John Brodie later played as a quarterback for the San Francisco 49ers. In 1964, Tony won the Bing Crosby National Pro-Am, the Thunderbird Classic, the Buick Open Invitational, and the Cleveland Open. He played the British Open at St. Andrews in 1964. He was persuaded by Arnold Palmer to play in this open. Palmer loaned him equipment to play plus his personal caddie. Tony Lema won, and the Scots called him the "Jolly Yank."

Tony was popular with the press. They liked his lively, witty, dramatic, and spontaneous interviews. In 1965 he was second to Jack Nicklaus in monies earned. His life was short, but people thought a lot about "Champagne Tony." One of Norman's friends, Manuel, a Portuguese in our group, knew Tony well. Manuel sold car parts to most of us who had cars at that time. This guy knew a lot of people that supplied parts to him for a price. I had heard that he came from a big family, all boys, in the 1950s. Many kids born in the 1930s had a lot of brothers. It seemed very common in the Latino families and the Italian, Portuguese, Mexican, and Irish families.

Once I had a 1940 Mercury sedan. Manuel sold me a complete clutch system and we took the car up to High Street to another guy that for a fee would put it in for you, bypassing the mechanics and their auto shops. Later on, through the big family of Anita's, I met other people that I knew. The family in the 1960s was truly a big family and we had a great time. Norman was one of my favorite cousins. Anita and I had a lot of fun with him in our early years. We double-dated and had a great time in Norman's lowered Chevy. It was a rough ride but we had a lot of fun riding around.

While working for the drugstore I would cut hair part-time to make some extra money. In the early 1960s, after working at the drugstore on the graveyard shift, they moved me to days. I now had a new boss, Harry Boyle. He ran the right side of the store. I would stock all the cosmetics, the sundries, the stationery, and the cards. We had four cosmetic people running the front departments. It was a good crew in the early '60s, and I learned a lot being on days. Harry was good to work for. He knew the business. Harry also knew a lot of the store and history of the company. One of the new experiences for me was the buying of cosmetics. I set up the inventory controls, the buying process, and the receiving procedures. The time went by fast each day. As the year passed I was helping out on the main floor, which was the promotional space in the center of the store. We had many a mid-shift during the time I spent helping Harry. We would come in at 2:00 p.m. and have an eight-hour shift, going home at 10:00 p.m. This three-shift system – morning, mid-shift, and graveyard – really helped. Inventories were difficult during the early years since it was all done by hand with no computers, and tallied the same way.

Harry once told me how the Skaggs family started the business. He said that our owner, L. J. Skaggs, came from a group of brothers that were store people who had started Skaggs United Stores, Safeway, Osco Drug, Sav-on Drugs, and our group, Pay-Less Drug Stores. The Skaggs family had helped Longs Drugs and Raley's get started back in the 1930s. I viewed this history as a young man and saw how this job could work out well for me

since I did not have a college background, only a good Catholic
school education. I put myself into learning as much as possible.
My goal was to be a manager someday.

Anita and I and Stevie were living with her mom and dad at
their place to save money to buy our own house some day. This
arrangement was the best thing for us. We saved a lot of money
with this arrangement. Working in Oakland at PayLess was great
because when I had no car, I would take the bus. It would leave
me right at the front door of the store. It was nice. The bus system
in Oakland ran on time. If you had no car, you could count on
the bus to get you to work on time.

The market at 1901 Telegraph Avenue was housed in an old
train terminal from the 1920s. Skaggs bought it and put his business in it. The building was divided, with a drugstore on the left
side and a grocery store on the right side. This was the main draw
to the site. Along the wall we had a meat counter by the front
door. Pucci Fish, Jim's BBQ, the Doughnut Shop, MacFarlane
Candy Company, and Davie's Meats were at the back with Joe's
Pizza and the George Brown Café. At the far back of the building we had our own warehouse and parking lot. Joe Dominaski
ran the parking lot.

By now you can visualize the stands we had. Each one had
to have its own owner. The stand owners had a lot of business
experience and they knew how to merchandise for the traffic and
sales volume. You need to visualize a ton of people shopping for
values. PayLess had a good concept. For example, the grocery
store would price eggs at thirty-nine cents a dozen, Scott brand
toilet paper at ten cents a roll, and make a profit, which is very
important if you are a retailer. The market would be busy all
week. PayLess Drug Stores ran weekly ads to draw people to the
location. As time passed I knew all the market people, some better than others, working at PayLess. The first year I did a lot of
stocking and buyer work at the pharmacy because of my experience at the Pill Hill pharmacy. I also did general merchandise
and lots of setups. In my fourth and fifth year I was given more

responsibilities and keys to the store, which meant a lot. I took all these responsibilities seriously, which helped me to be recognized as a company man. I had expressed to upper management that I wanted to be a manager.

My manager, Bill Gherra, was behind my career goal to move up in due time. He was well-known in the business and highly respected by Mr. Skaggs. Bill Gherra finally moved to the main office as president of PayLess Drug Stores. I had met Mr. Gherra when I was a barber at the Key Barber Shop in Emeryville. He gave me the job at PayLess Drug Store. When Bill Gherra took the office of president in the 1960s and 1970s we started the plan to grow and build stores in the outlying areas. We still had four stores in the mid 1960s and 1970s. So the potential was there for me to move up. Going back to the people you meet at work or throughout the market was an experience of understanding each person.

One of the stands was a chicken stand. This stand sold fresh eggs, chicken, chicken parts, sausages, pizza, barbecue items, salads, and other items. The owner was Jim Gangle. Jim was about five foot eight. He was built solid with a dark complexion. He was an Italian Sicilian. Jim was a believer in honesty, honor, integrity, and loyalty. I respected Jim all the years we worked in Oakland at 1901 Telegraph Avenue. I would buy my lunch at this stand. He sold the best barbecue chicken. The only other barbecue chicken I had tasted was on Ninth and Broadway. The spices they put on the chicken while cooking it makes the difference. As time passed, Jim and I became good friends. I really liked Jim, and I liked his approach to matters. I was in my early twenties. Jim must have been ten years older. Jim worked his stand with his wife and family. They were all good people.

The market people were characters. Some had quarrels that they expressed openly at the market for all to hear. Once when I was in charge of the store, we had a big commotion at the butcher shop in front by the door. What happened was this: the German owner had gone back to his icebox and was drinking. His wife got so mad at him that when he came out to the front counter, she started throwing the big rolls of bologna and salami at him. They were fighting it out beside their stand, belting each other, fighting and cursing so the customers entering could not miss it. The customers were shocked but laughing as they walked around them.

Like I said, the market had its stories. But in these times people didn't talk about it. The two people who were having the fight just did what they did. They reacted how they felt, pulling no punches. For them, it was fighting time and the others just let them be. The next day the couple were like two love doves.

FIVE

Becoming a Company Man

In the early 1960s, the growth of PayLess Drug Stores was going as planned. And I was gaining more experience. One of the things that happened to me was working with a lot of young people my age because the company was in need of talent. Some of the older employees or guys were about ten years older. These older people were being moved up. This gave us twenty-year-olds a chance to replace them. When I was about twenty-five, PayLess sold the market. It was prime real estate. They got about one or two million dollars. We needed the money to grow as a company. I was offered a promotion as a supervisor to move to Pleasant Hills PayLess. I discussed it with Anita. We both decided it was a good move for her and me. One of the big things was our plan to look somewhere for a house to buy. So the move gave us a chance to look and buy. In the meantime we lived with Anita's parents, Mae and Bill. I believe I drove from Mae and Bill's house to Pleasant Hill for about a year.

The store in Pleasant Hill was a large store. It had opened in the early 1960s and was a winner. It had a lot of profit. The store had a big nursery, a big drugstore, and general merchandise. I was in a new environment compared to the old market. Jim Gangle opened a barbecue stand at the front lobby of the drugstore. His

nephew ran it. I did see Jim quite often. It was always good to
see him. Jim would ask how my family and I were doing. Jim was
still at the old market at 1901 Telegraph. He would say the place
was the same but the people were getting ready to close shop. Jim
said he would open a big barbecue place in the Mountain View
PayLess location. His barbecue would be on the grocery lobby
side near the food store side. He mentioned to me that, Leo, his
brother-in-law, was opening his own barbecue place at the Pay-
Less Drug Store on Prospect in Campbell, a good location. I knew
Jim would do well in his three new locations, now that he had to
close at 1901 Telegraph Avenue.

While still working at the Pleasant Hill store, I received from
Mr. Gherra assurance that it would be a good time to buy a home.
Anita and I did not want to buy for our current location if there
was a possibility of a transfer. Anita came out to Pleasant Hill. We
found a place for $15,000 in an established section of the town
of Concord. After putting down the money, would you believe
PayLess asked me to be an assistant manager at a store, and we
would have to move! I called Mr. Gherra and explained to him
that we were in the process of buying. He said to see what I could
do to get out of it. The company would pay the losses. We did
get out of the transaction, but the promotion was put on hold. So
we decided to reapply to buy again. This time we found a nice
place in Concord, though it was a little more than the first house.
I spent about three to four years at the Pleasant Hill store. This
place had a good volume and was a good profit store.

Anita: Our house in Concord was our first home purchase and move. It
wasn't so bad. The only problem was I didn't drive at the time, and that
was hard. We moved in, and the next weekend they pulled Ruben to open
another store in another area. And Ruben expected me to introduce
myself to the neighbor and ask them if they could take me shopping. I
was very shy at that young age, and this just wasn't going to happen.
So there I was getting settled with the boys, Steve and Willie. Steve was

the only one in school at the time, and Wally wasn't born yet. After some time in Concord we were again expecting.

But I had still not learned to drive, and my doctor was in San Leandro. Needless to say, being young and irresponsible, Ruben hadn't put gas in the car. Now tell me, what man doesn't have a car gassed up at all times when he has a wife at home ready to deliver a child? Not my hubby. But it all worked out, and all survived, and we had our third boy, Wally.☆

In the middle 1960s, the Pleasant Hill store continued to have good sales volume. I became a second assistant manager there. This was a promotion. The promotion that was put on hold was out of town and I would have been a first assistant manager, leading up to manager. With the new responsibility, I learned more, and I still had my strong desire to be a manager. Anita had her hands full with a grade school student, a preschooler, and then our new little guy, Wally. Anita worked hard to be a good mother and wife. I was putting a lot of time into my job. Sometimes I wasted hours on my foolishness of going out with the boys for beer time. How she put up with this type of behavior, I don't know. I am glad she had the understanding and love for me to keep going. She is a great wife.

In the late 1960s Mr. Gherra asked me to move to the new store coming up in San Pablo. San Pablo is closer to Oakland. About this same time the Black Panthers group was coming alive in West Oakland. What PayLess offered was the first assistant manager job, under the manager, Walter Chinn, in San Pablo. This store was a new store layout for PayLess. It was a huge store, about 57,000 square feet with a major appliance department.

I did not move Anita and our boys right away. I could drive from Concord on the San Pablo Dam Road right to the San Pablo store. By now we had Wally, born summer 1966, in San Leandro Memorial Hospital. During the late 1960s Dad died. In 1967 Mom was still on Seventh Street. The shop was closed down. Mom's old house wasn't on the schedule to be torn down yet, but she was getting ready to move. All of West Oakland and Seventh Street to the Point was being torn down for the new freeway and big post office. There was a lot going on in this time period, not only with me but also with my mom and the West Oakland situation about her house. The company had sent me to open the San Pablo store to gain that experience for the future. The store was in a rough neighborhood. It was also at a cross street with good freeway access to the Dam Road. The Richmond branch of the Panthers was also targeting the PayLess Stores just to be a nuisance. We had a tough time in this store. In the 1970s the Oakland chapter of the Black Panthers was putting the Oakland police on notice because of the brutality the police used on the citizens. The police had been brutal, I knew, from times past in old West Oakland. The Black Panthers under leader Huey P. Newton crafted a Ten Point Program that stated their demands. He wanted power to determine the future for the Black community.

This movement had a big effect on the white, Chinese, and Latino cultures in Oakland and surrounding areas. The Panthers had its headquarters close to my dad's old shop. With this activity and all the changes with the post office and freeway, it was good that Mom was closing down and moving.

I had joined the National Guard in the middle of the 1960s with a lot of old neighborhood friends: Tommy Cheveres, Pete Escovedo, Al Larios, Victor Lara, Manuel Escovedo, Gomez, and others. We all signed up for three years. We would meet at Pete Escovedo's mom's place and drive to Richmond for our meeting at the armory. The group was a lot of fun. Tommy was the center of keeping it a fun time. Once a year we had to go to Camp Roberts for ground training for two weeks. We lived in barracks next to the regular army. It was okay but it's not like home. I finished my three years of duty and was proud that I served. Most people think that being in the reserves is not serving. The Korean conflict had stopped before our time in the National Guard. Otherwise we all could have been called into the regular army.

I learned a lot more about PayLess, about retail, and about

myself, working for Mr. Walt Chinn. I now knew a lot of store managers, vendors, PayLess main office people, and other people in other stores. Chinn was the manager recognized for his loyalty, detail of planning, organizing, implementing, and ad coordination for the Bay Area, controlling and putting programs on paper for others to understand. The San Pablo store was the Bay Area contact for newspaper ad selections. I was one of the contact people for the vendors and saw them every week. I also had to take a lot of responsibility off Mr. Chinn by being in charge of the store. The ad preparation took a lot of his time. I worked well with Walt Chinn. He taught me a lot about the business, especially how to read the store's financial statements, which most managers did not understand. One thing that took a toll on me was the extra hours that Walt worked. This part was hard on the off-clock crew and me. Walt was generous to his key people. At Christmas time he took care of us. My first Christmas working for him, he gave me this heavy box all wrapped up. I took it home. Anita and I opened it up. There was a big ham leg. It weighed at least twenty to thirty pounds. It was a surprise but we enjoyed it right to the bone.

During this time, a lot of things were changing for me. I had finally reached my goal of getting close to being a manager. As I look back, I realize I made a big mistake. The focus was 90 percent on the job and my desire to get ahead. I was doing well for being with the company ten to twelve years. But in doing this, I neglected Anita and my boys. Anita is a special person. She had a valid reason to call it quits. But she did not, and today while writing this, I see my mistake of being blinded by my goal of succeeding.

I saw my friend Jim Gangle once in San Pablo. He was looking at a location in our store. But it was too small for his operation. I asked Jim if he knew Joe from the Big Red Barn or Crabby Joe's Big Barn in Oakland. He said he knew Joe from the old days in Oakland and that Joe had a new place in Jack London Square. Jim said Joe was a connected guy who always was active in unusual business ventures. But Joe's situation has changed since the war ended. Jim said during the war Joe and his business had a good thing with the Western dance bars in Oakland and North Oakland. I can remember how the southerners who came to Oakland liked their Western music. Some of Anita's cousins married what we would call Okies. They worked at the clubs in San Pablo Avenue as bouncers at the door. This is a story in itself. Jim knew a lot of the story of San Francisco and Oakland of the 1930s to 1940 war years. Jim gave me a lot of good advice, and I am glad to have had it as a young man.

The San Pablo store started out slow. We had to really think of ways to get people into our store. The locals took a long time to give us a chance. Our location had good parking and the prices were good. Next door we also had an Albertsons grocery store.

In 1967, Anita and I sold our home in Concord to move to 150th Avenue near Goat Hill in San Leandro. We bought a newly built home, as did Anita's mom and dad. In fact they bought the home right next door. Now my drive to San Pablo became easier. My drive to work went from 150th Avenue to San Pablo Dam Road. It was a straight shot on the freeway that ran along the Oakland Hills. My mom had bought a home on Thirty-Seventh Avenue behind St. Elizabeth High School in East Oakland. This was a little place with one bedroom, a small kitchen, and a small front room. The good thing was that now she was surrounded by family, especially my sister Juanita. Many grandchildren and other family members were able to visit. Mom now was aging. The years were showing. Her hair was all gray. She was a good-looking lady with nice features. In one of the albums I put together, you can see what a beautiful lady she was. Mom always kept herself neat and clean. As a child, I remember her keeping us neat and clean.

Anita: A few short years after the move to Concord, we had a home built on 150th Avenue. This was in San Leandro at the bottom of what people referred to as Goat Hill or Okie Hill. My parents lived next door to us, and Mom—that is, my mom—was in and out of the hospital. We lived here before our move to Southern California. And Ruben worked in San Pablo. It wasn't so bad here. I had most of my relatives living around us at this time. So I actually enjoyed it. I always loved being around my fun-loving Puerto Rican family. And we weren't far from the Portuguese side of the family on my dad's side. From this home we did the next big move: this time to Southern California. ✖

I once thought while working in San Pablo about all the time I had with PayLess. It was now ten years. I became disappointed when I began to realize that people with fewer years were being promoted to manager. Somewhere in the late 1960s, Mr. Gherra had come by the store to visit. I asked him to meet with me, which he agreed to do. I sat down with Mr. Gherra, who by now was the chairman of the board of PayLess Drug Stores. I explained to him that I felt slighted by all the promotions to manager for people who had less seniority than I had. He said I needed to be patient and that he would take care of me. I believed him. Later, around 1968 or 1970, he called me and asked me to accept a store in Lakewood, California. This store was outside Long Beach, in Southern California. I accepted the manager job at thirty-one years of age. I would go to the Los Angeles area and be working for a district manager by the name of Jim Steel. I knew Jim Steel through the years. As I did, he attended all the seasonal shows we put together for the company at our store in San Pablo, California.

Anita and I now had to leave all our families to move again. We bought a large two-story home in Cerritos, near Long Beach. My drive to work was an easy one. Anita made the house up. We all lived there: the three boys and Anita's parents, Nana and Pop. We spent about three years in Cerritos. A lot of family from the Bay Area did come down. We were less than three miles from Disneyland, so you can see why it seemed we always had company around.

Anita: When we moved to Southern California, Ruben went ahead and I stayed behind and sold the house. We were very excited and really looked forward to it. My mother and father also were moving in with us at that time also. My mom wasn't a very healthy person. And I was always there to help my dad take care of her. The boys were also excited once they found out we were going to be near Disneyland. The problem was our house didn't sell for months. I believe it was at least eight months. It was miserable for all of us. We did fly back and forth and finally found a great home. It was by far my favorite home ever. I loved the spacious rooms. And we had room for the boys and my parents. It was very modern and had a large balcony off the master bedroom—such a great home.

Cerritos was everything we expected, with a lot of fun things to do. The boys made friends easily and Steve was going to graduate from the newly built high school. Many of the family members used to visit. One New Year's Eve about 11:30 we had about five cars of family surprise us. We had wall-to-wall people. It was crazy, but fun. Besides Disneyland, we had the Japanese Deer Park and Knott's Berry Farm to take the family to see. We had so much to do there, and we truly enjoyed living there. Many of the relatives stayed with us while they took in the sights.

My Uncle Peter made his first visit to Disneyland, and he was so amazed with Mr. Lincoln. He couldn't get over the fact that a mannequin was delivering the speech. He was so cute talking about it.

Another time my Uncle George had a heart attack while staying at the Disneyland Hotel. After he was released from the hospital, my aunt and he stayed with us when he recovered until the doctor released him to go back to the Bay Area, where they lived. We were happy to help them. ✵

Our PayLess Store in Lakewood was a big store. We had all the merchandise that our stores had in the northern part of California. The problem in Southern California was that our stores were spread out so far from each other. This made it hard for people to know us or to locate a PayLess Drug Store near them. In the Los Angeles area, Sav-on Drugs had many more locations and people were used to them and knew where they were. About the time I opened the Lakewood PayLess Drug Store, PayLess had bought some stores in Hawaii. The Hawaii stores were having problems. The stores in the Los Angeles area also were having volume problems. That was a big change for me. The company was expecting a lot from the Southern California managers. It was not easy to put a plan together when our stores were so far apart.

Sometime around 1973 Roy Martin, who had been promoted to president of the retail stores, came by to see me in the Lakewood store. He needed a strong manager in the store at Mountain View in the San Francisco Bay Area, which had a volume of sales greater than all the other California stores. Plus it was a very profitable store. The manager would make a big bonus of $20,000 or more, plus salary. Anita and I discussed this move. The bonus was a big plus in motivating us to move.

During our stay in Cerritos, Anita developed cancer in one of her breasts, which was removed. Anita had to make a tough decision on that one. It was not easy for her. But she is very strong and made that tough decision. We did the surgery and moved ahead with our lives. I am glad that she handled it so well. That is her . . . never give up . . . get moving forward.

Anita: I liked living in Cerritos. We had good neighbors and a nice house. Nana and Pop were enjoying it there. It seemed like the boys were enjoying the area. We must have been in Cerritos for about four years.

We made a few lifetime friends that we still keep in touch with. After about three or four years Ruben came home from work and told us, "They want me to take over the Mountain View store." I think I cried with the boys this time. We were so comfortable living here. The big shock was they wanted to know by the next day! Who does that to families? Corporations, that's who! Anyway, they made us an offer Ruben couldn't refuse.

So Ruben was off again and I had to deal with selling the house and the boys being very, very upset. I had an appointment with a doctor the next day after Ruben flew to San Jose to report to the Mountain View store. The big shocker was I learned that I had to have a breast removed. So, he was in Mountain View and I was in Southern California—and facing cancer surgery at my young age of just reaching the thirties. And I was so lucky to have my loving parents living with me at that time. I really needed the support.

It was not the best time in our lives. The boys were miserable and so was I. Ruben did fly home for my surgery. I did see him before the surgery. But he left too soon. I felt he should have stayed another day or so. I didn't remember him being there when I came out of recovery. That really hurt.

The transfer years weren't happy ones in our marriage or life as a family. The boys and I had a lot to deal with. Our eldest son, Stephen, must have attended six different schools. We always accepted the transfers because I didn't want to feel I was holding Ruben back from advancement with the company. And they always promised better wages. What a bunch of poppycock! The people who never accepted the transfers moved just as fast if not faster than the ones who did. You can be so naïve when you are as young as we were at the time. We lost money with every move we made, so nothing was really gained.

Once again we made it through. But I was holding it against him. And this was not good. I started to resent him and the company. I hated to have to sell the home I loved and to leave the friends I had made. I know it was just a house. But to me it was more. We were really happy there. And wouldn't you know it: the house didn't sell fast. President Nixon put the freeze on everything and everyone tightened their belts. Ruben did fly home as much as he could. A couple of times a month. ✴

We decided to move to east San Jose into another large two-story home. The home was in a new development. With all our boys, Nana and Pop, we needed more room. The boys were growing up and they needed some privacy for themselves. We really lucked out. We had good neighbors. They were a lot of fun. Anita again worked on getting the house livable and did her thing to make it nice. Anita and her dad did a great job landscaping the yard. It was beautiful. They put in a corner waterfall. You could hear the water running at night. It was great. The neighborhood had a lot of boys who were around the ages of our boys so they had a lot of kids to play with. This move put us closer to the family we had in Oakland. They would come out to see us. For me to go to work in Mountain View was an easy drive. Our situation on finances got better for Anita and me. We were able to buy me a better car to drive. The old Ford was not reliable, as it was down to its last miles.

The stay in San Jose was about four or five years. In Mountain View I was able to meet up with Jim Gangle and his wife, Dorothy. They had a big barbecue stand near an Albertsons. Until we got settled I was living in an apartment behind the store. I did this for about seven months. The delay resulted from President Nixon putting a freeze on all pricing, including pay raises, in the United States. Real estate and other financial matters, just about everything, slowed down.

Down in Southern California, Anita could not sell the new Cerritos home. Buyers were only looking, not buying. The home sale market was dead. The Gangles would have me over for dinner regularly. I really got to know both of them. At the apartment I had a friend named Paul Kantner. He and his friend Edna would visit, have some drinks and talk. Paul's son is a famous musician from the 1960s and 1970s. His son's band was Jefferson Airplane. His partner at the time was Grace Slick. They had a daughter, China Kantner.

Paul was a salesperson for one of the Skaggs family's distributors. I had worked with Paul for maybe fourteen years in the Bay Area. Getting to know him in Mountain View was great. The visits we had at the apartment were very helpful to me. Paul had a lot of good advice. Up to this time I did not know that Paul had a son or anything else. Paul during this time must have been in his eighties. Still he was sharp, as was Edna, who was also up in age. They were good people. Anita would come up for a visit when she could, and she got to know them also.

Anita: We finally sold the house and purchased a home in San Jose, California. The boys were enrolled in the new schools, and there was a lot of bitterness at first, which I caught the brunt of because I was home to hear it all. We made new friends and so did the boys. And it turned out to be a really nice place to live. Dad and I created some pretty neat yards. I still liked Cerritos best! But it was fun to create things. I did a lot of wallpapering and painting. I also did a lot of sewing in those days. This was fun for me. I always enjoyed creating pretty things. That's probably what helped in my floral design, and finally opening my own shop . . . after, you guessed it, one more move. �֍

The Mountain View store needed a lot of my time. When I got there the place was a mess. All control was gone. They had no leadership. The manager before me had given up. I had worked with Bill Howard in Pleasant Hill. Bill was a good PR man, one of the best. He was a first assistant at Pleasant Hill. I was his second assistant. I had the brunt of work, and I did it. I liked Bill so it was okay. He was good to me. So I let him do the PR, and the mix was good. What had happened to him in Mountain View was allowing his team to do whatever they wanted and not holding them accountable. The other thing was his wife was ill, and she died. I knew Helen. She was a good person. I believe Bill gave up because of such a loss. The company removed him, and I replaced Bill in Mountain View. I did learn later somewhere along the line that Bill moved to Carmel-by-the-Sea and opened a golf shop. Some said he and Clint Eastwood would golf together, even in his golf store. I could see that Bill was the best in PR, and people liked him. I had worked with his mom in Oakland. They were good people.

In 1976 the company was pleased with the turnaround of the Mountain View store and its improvements. The company asked me to become a vice president of the Central California Division of PayLess Drug Stores. I would be responsible for stores from Reno to Tahoe to Bakersfield. I accepted the promotion, and Anita again started the search for a new home, this time in Sacramento.

Anita: Again after three or four years Ruben was promoted to be one of the vice presidents of PayLess Drug Stores and was sent to the Sacramento home office. And this meant we had to move again. This was okay. Stephen was in the Navy, but Willie wasn't happy about it, and neither was Wally. But we eventually accepted the transfer. But I also made it clear that if he accepted another transfer he would be moving ALONE! Enough was enough.✵

During this period I was handling my new responsibility of covering all these stores from Reno to Bakersfield. While doing this new job I had a medical emergency. My chronic back problem became an instant emergency. All my years of commuting and driving finally got to me. I knew my usual pain, but this was extreme. I needed medical attention at once. I was in Sacramento, and Anita was in San Jose. I decided to drive to San Jose for this medical attention. It was a big mistake. The long drive just made the pain more intense. I did make it to San Jose. But I was a wreck. The pain was so intense I cried while I was driving. I could not get out of the car. The doctor looked at me. After the examination he told me that he needed to operate on my back at once. He told me the chances were that I could end up in a wheelchair if I didn't have this operation. He gave me time to call Anita and Mr. Gherra to tell them where I was. Anita came right over to the hospital. This experience was the worst time for me. I had never felt such pain that was so intense.

Anita: While we were still in San Jose, Ruben had to have emergency surgery. He was already working in Sacramento and decided to drive home to San Jose. The pain was overwhelming and he drove straight to the hospital. At that time he called me, and they took him to the operating room. I don't even remember if I got to see him before the surgery. The doctor didn't know if he would be able to walk after the surgery. We have been blessed through all of this. He could walk, and we are still together after fifty-five years, and we have three wonderful sons and their great families. Sometimes you have to put your feelings aside and take the plunge.✵

After surgery I had to take it easy. The doctor felt it would be a year before I would feel better. The time off might have been three months. I needed to work. I had just received this promotion. I worked as the vice president of store operations about two years. The driving became an issue. My back could not handle the long drive. I would be stiff as a board when arriving at my destination. In December of 1978, I notified the company that I was resigning as vice president of store operations. They were good about it. They suggested I take a local store in Sacramento. I decided to go back to being a store manager at the Citrus Heights store. In 1980, PayLess Drug Stores was bought by PayLess Northwest, out of Oregon. The next two years, changes were implemented. They had new programs, and you needed to follow them 100 percent. The changes were harder to implement in our stores. We did not have discipline. The PayLess company I knew never had all the micromanagement rules. After four years at the store, I resigned from PayLess, after twenty-six years. I was tired. I needed a change. So I quit.

Anita and I opened a full-line florist shop on Watt and Arden. The shop was between Albertsons and a PayLess Drug Store. We did well. Anita and her crew made up the arrangements. My job was to go to the San Francisco Flower Market and buy our supplies and drive them back to Sacramento by 6 a.m. The shop did well. Anita knew this business. She made the shop a success. Anita is a good businessperson; she taught me a lot. About the time our lease was up, her dad became ill with cancer. Anita decided we would sell the shop. We did sell at once. The location was good and parking was great.

Anita brought her dad home so she could take care of him. I found a manager's job with a company called Pic 'N' Save. I worked as a manager for them for twenty-one years. I left them at the end of December 2009, for a new adventure. PayLess Drug Stores, the company I gave most of my youth to, was bought up by Kmart, Thrifty, and now at this time is called Rite Aid. Anita's dad, Pop, died at home with his grandson Willie, his wife Mae, and his daughter Anita by his side. Mae also lived with us in her old age until she needed a medical home. This home was across from the American River College. She died there.

We continue living in Carmichael. Our son, Willie Llamas, got sick and we brought him home to live with us to help him overcome his cancer of the throat. He received chemo, radiation, and fifteen or more surgeries. At this time of writing, 2012, he is doing okay. We all know he is in fourth stage of this cancer and that he will have little chance to overcome it if it comes back. He is a positive person and has never complained of his sickness. I admire him for that. We all want the best for him.

Aside from our worries about Willie, Anita and I are happy. We have a solid, good family. We have had our share of life's detours. The big thing is not to give up. Deal with it in your way and keep going forward. You believe in the Lord; it will work out. But you have to accept your condition. Then do something to make it right for you. It will make you a better person!

Well, that is most of my life. I leave this to you to know where we came from and what a great country we live in: the United States of America is still the place of opportunities. You have to make it happen. So do something to improve your life and family.

Ruben and
Anita's boys,
Willie, Steve,
and Wally
(clockwise from
top).

Jim Gangle, a mentor and friend of the family.

PayLess Drug Store, 1901 Telegraph Avenue, Oakland.

PART TWO
Looking Lively:
West Oakland's Sports and Music

Carl "Bobo" Olson, World Middleweight Boxing Champion, with his belt.

Overleaf: Ruben's mother, Sara Llamas, with Carl "Bobo" Olson, World Middleweight Boxing Champion, at a family event.

SIX

Boxing in Oakland

———◆◆◆◆———

Boxing in Oakland had been a popular sport since the 1930s. Promoters of prizefights often used the Oakland Auditorium at Lake Merritt. Oakland had many a prizefight. Wednesday was the "Fight Night." Many neighborhoods put up a fighter to see who could produce the best boxer. West Oakland in the old days had Battling Benny Vierra, and Bobby Dalton who fought under the name of "Bobby Burns." Other local boxers were outstanding also.

One of these local boxers was a West Oakland boy, Art Garcia. He fought all over the Bay Area. I met the Garcias in the early 1950s. When I attended Westlake School up on Harrison, I met Art's brother, Robert Garcia, who I knew from the neighborhood. Art Garcia was a good boxer with discipline who was in control of his fights. A good boxer knew the ring. His brother, Stanley, in later years founded the East Oakland Boxing Association to give young people hope and skills for the future. He did a lot for the East Oakland kids. Stanley was a life coach to the kids, and his guidance was lifesaving. He was dedicated to the inner city kids and to developing their minds and bodies. His work at the gym touched a lot of people. Stanley Garcia passed away at the age of sixty.

103

Ruben's personal picture from Carl "Bobo" Olson with Max Baer, Carl in the middle, and the favorite, Joe Louis. These guys had heart.

These Garcia boys did a lot of boxing at the Oakland Auditorium, the Oakland Army Terminal, the San Francisco Civic Auditorium, and the Ringside Boxing Club. I knew them from the neighborhood in West Oakland through the sports we played. You met a lot of kids: boxers, football and baseball players, and other sportsmen. You would see the young kids at different events and they would associate you with being from the same neighborhood. Also lots of kids came by my dad's La Ideal Music Shop. One of their brothers I also knew by going to Westlake High School. When they moved to East Oakland next to the Greyhound depot on East Fourteenth Street, I would see them. I also saw them at Babe's Gym on East Fourteenth Street.

Oakland boy Johnny Gonsalves and the Garcia Brothers, Art and Stanley, were among the best. Most of the local boxers had local boxing gyms for training. Downtown we had Duffy's Gym at 424 Eleventh Street, directly across the street from the T&D Theater. It was the gym where Jim Dundee and Harold Broom worked out. Max Baer was a regular at this gym. He was from Livermore. In West Oakland they had a gym called the Yosemite Athletic Club at 500 Union Street at Fifth Street. The West Oakland boxers would go there to train. Harold Broom ran the gym at 534 Twentieth Street. It was called Imperial Athletic Club. Harold was known as the best trainer in the Bay Area. In East Oakland right off Fruitvale and East Fourteenth Street, the gym called Babe's was where Johnny Gonsalves and other boxers trained. The city in the 1930s to the 1960s had a lot of young kids that wanted to be boxers. The kids saw boxing as a way out of the West Oakland environment. The street life was tough. Boxing opened up the door to growing as a person with the discipline, maturity, and development your mind and your body needed to make it. Training a boxer is a commitment between him and the trainer to develop the skills for winning.

Some of the kids started boxing while we were in school. St. Mary's parish had a boxing gym below the school building. The Holy Name sisters would not let you go to the gym during the school session – only after school when a trainer was there. This gym was Father John Ralph Duggan's idea. He had the basement under the school rearranged for a boxing gym. It was to keep the kids busy and away from the pachuco gangs of the neighborhood. Father Duggan did a great job of starting many athletic teams to keep the young people busy. I can remember many a kid getting help in boxing training from other young boxers to prepare them for the sport. Lots of kids learned to box just for the sake of it. They didn't go on to competitive boxing but the skills of boxing helped them be better people by learning discipline and how to fight by the rules.

St. Mary's boxing program had a trainer to guide the new boxers. One of the young trainers was Jimmy Delgadillo, himself a young boxer. Also many police officers who knew Father Duggan helped with all the athletic programs. Father helped a lot of kids get into sports, such as swimming at local schools or the Oakland Estuary, the Catholic Youth Organization/United Services Organization, or the Jewish Community Center, YMCA, and the Downtown Club or the Hayward Plunge. He established sandlot baseball teams. The teams played in various leagues around Oakland, including the Oakland Police League. Father Duggan would also put on fight programs in the school auditorium. These fight nights were busy matches with the local young boxers in West Oakland. The trainers were Oakland policemen. They put on a good show. The place was always packed. They must have had a lot of promoters around. The boxers in the four rounders really punched it out. The fighters took a beating, and the crowd loved it. The boxers showed the skills needed to survive the beatings.

In the early 1950s, boxing in Oakland was big-time. The shows were at the Ringside Boxing Club, Oakland Auditorium, Army Terminal, and San Francisco Auditorium, but the boxers often trained at our gym. While I was going to St. Elizabeth High School, I met a kid, Brian, who would take us down to Babe's Gym to watch the boxers coming up. Our local guy, Johnny Gonsalves, was a lightweight boxer, a good foot man, and a counterpuncher.

Johnny had a big following in Oakland. He was a Portuguese kid from the local neighborhood. Brian's dad, Jack, was his manager. So going down to Babe's Gym was an easy way to see some good boxing.

During the whole period of the late 1930s through the 1960s, boxing had a big following, with big fights at the Oakland Auditorium. I remember buying *The Ring* magazine to see the pictures of my favorite boxers. We would listen to the radio if the fight was broadcast, and then watch a TV set with a black-and-white screen in the early 1940s and 1950s: TV was just reaching the public. The fighters were strong, tough, and had a lot of heart. Some of the boxers I remember are Sugar Ray Robinson, Jake LaMotta, Rocky Graziano, Tony Zale, Willie Pep, Robert Duran, Sal Bartolo, Jersey Joe Walcott, Ezzard Charles, Kid Gavilán, Cassius Clay (before he changed his name to Muhammad Ali), Ingemar Johansson, Joey Giardello, Gene Fullmer, Carmen Basilio, Archie Moore, Floyd Patterson, and my favorites Joe Louis, Max Baer, Carl "Bobo" Olson, and Rocky Marciano, a heavyweight who was undefeated.

Years later after Anita and I moved to Sacramento, I met Carl "Bobo" Olson again, and we became friends in Rancho Cordova where he lived. At the time I was manager for Big Lots in Rancho Cordova. In the Oakland neighborhood I knew of Carl because Uncle Johnny on Twenty-Third Avenue would cut his hair. He was family. Bill Garcia, my father-in-law, knew Bobo from Hawaii as well as from Twenty-Third Avenue in Oakland.

Bobo was born in Honolulu, Hawaii, to a Portuguese mother and Swedish father. He learned at a young age to box from his street fights in a tough downtown area. Honolulu was his training time. He was in Hawaii during World War II when he would bump into drunken soldiers on the street and have to fight back when they picked fights. Carl began fighting professionally at age sixteen. He spent endless days lifting weights, running, and sparring. He won nineteen fights before he reached the age where he could legally box on the mainland circuit. As a professional,

Bobo won the World Middleweight Championship by defeating Randy Turpin of England in October 1953. After three years or so Bobo Olson fought Robinson for the title. On December 9, 1955, Olson put his title on the line against Sugar Ray Robinson. Olson was favored in this bout but was knocked out in the second round. Sugar Ray won, by decision. Olson fought Sugar Ray again in a rematch; Bobo was knocked out in the fourth round. Soon after, Olson announced his retirement as a middleweight. His record was 97 wins, 47 by KO (knock out), 16 losses, and 2 draws. Bobo is known as a former World Middleweight Boxing Champ, holding the title for three years before relinquishing it to Sugar Ray in 1956. Bobo continued to fight, this time in the light heavyweight classification. He toured Europe, South Africa, and the United States. He retired in 1966 after he had worked himself up to be the number one light heavyweight contender.

After retiring from professional boxing, Bobo worked as a recreational director for the Operating Engineers Local Union No. 3 headquartered in San Francisco. He managed the recreational facilities at Local 3's Rancho Murieta Training Center, near Sacramento. The fellows studying for the construction business at this somewhat isolated training center enjoyed not only a gym but a boxing ring plus the training expertise of a retired champion boxer. Bobo recommended rising early in the morning and running right away. But instead of jogging steadily, he advised future boxers to vary the speed: sprint, then slow down, sprint some more, then slow down. This method develops your wind for the on-off situation that boxing demands. He also recommended a healthful diet: a good breakfast after the morning run; a small lunch of salad or a sandwich; then a good dinner but no more food before going to bed.

Carl "Bobo" Olson would come to my Rancho Cordova Big Lots store to see me. We would talk and visit. He had a good heart; he was a good person and an upstanding guy. Our family loved Bobo Olson. I am glad I got to know him and his family.

Bobo died January 16, 2002, after living into his mid-seventies, a long life for a boxing champ.

My other favorite boxer was Joe Louis. We didn't know him the way we knew Bobo. But Joe Louis was an American hero to all of us. He, an African American, was challenged to fight a German boxer of Hitler's choice. Hitler was sure the Aryan German would win. But Joe Louis won, and all of us in America were very proud. Joe Louis remains an American hero to this day.

Lalo Guerrero (third from left) visited Ruben's father at the music shop.

Ruben's father and brother Mario (back row center) in La Ideal Music Shop with the Saturday night regulars.

110

SEVEN

Music and Dance in West Oakland

Mexican culture has always included a love of music with a distinct musical sound. When my folks were young they must have heard the music of the ranchera, the mariachi, and the corrido, such as you would hear in the rural areas and the urban outskirts. Young men would try to capture the heart of a young señorita with their singing and guitar playing of soft romantic ballads.

The music in West Oakland had this flavor and much more. With my dad's La Ideal Music Shop, music was a very important part of our lives, even if we ourselves didn't play musical instruments. Many musicians both local and national, when they were in town, came to him to discuss the music of the times. Dad would sell the recordings of all these well-known singers and musicians. He would make sure they knew the hot stuff and the old stuff. They kept him up-to-date and he kept others up-to-date.

Pedro Infante

Pedro was a Mexican singer and film star of the 1940s and 1950s. This period was the golden age of Mexican cinema, and Pedro was the idol of the Mexican people. He was born on November 18, 1917, at Mazatlán, Sinaloa, Mexico. By 1939 he had appeared in

111

more than sixty films, and since 1943 he had recorded 350 songs. In the late 1940s and mid 1950s, promoters would bring him to Oakland to entertain the Mexican people throughout the Bay Area. Anytime Pedro came to Oakland he stayed at the Leamington Hotel, a fashionable hotel in Oakland. Then Pedro would do something else. He would call Dad to have my mother, Sarita, cook him a meal at our house. I remember this big honor for all of us to have this idol come to the house. Mom had no problem recruiting the ladies to help her prepare this special meal. Mom did a lot of cooking in this time of her life. Later on she did not cook such big meals. My mom and her lady friends would put together a grand Mexican meal. We all loved to see Pedro!

But for my dad, seeing Pedro was like seeing a brother or sister. They would give each other the *abrazo*, a special greeting – an embrace – for special people. One reason Pedro and my dad were so close was because Dad was from Pedro's birth area, Mazatlán. Pedro also took time to talk to us kids. He was a very special person to us, not just because he was a famous star, but because we knew he really liked to see us and our family.

I have a lot of fun pictures of these dinners and a ton of good memories. We were very sad when Pedro Infante died April 15, 1957, in an air crash at Mérida, Yucatán, Mexico. He was mourned by all the people who loved him. Even the young Mexican Americans today know about this special actor and singer.

Lalo Guerrero

Another nationally known singer and songwriter I must mention is Lalo Guerrero. He was not as close a family friend as Pedro Infante, or as locally involved as Guadalupe Carlos, who I describe more fully a few pages later. But Eduardo "Lalo" Guerrero was known nationally as the father of Chicano music. Lalo was honored for this role in a variety of ways. He gained notice in 1955 for a parody of "The Ballad of Davy Crockett." The Smithsonian Institution named him a National Folk Treasure. President Clinton recognized Lalo in 1997 by bestowing on him the National Medal of Arts in company with Lionel Hampton, Robert Redford, Stephen Sondheim, and Edward Albee. Lalo both wrote and sang songs with remarkable range and a social conscience. He performed hundreds of benefit concerts a year, and was a friend of labor hero César Chávez. In the Coachella Valley he was best known as a song parodist. He also wrote several pachuco songs that became popular in the 1979 musical *Zoot Suit*, which started his international touring. Lalo Guerrero died in 2005 at the age of 88.

West Oakland Musical Hot Spots

Sweets Ballroom was built by a wealthy Oakland resident, Mr. Hassler, as an investment. It was begun in September of 1923 and finished in March of 1924 at a cost of $80,000. Since 1924, William Sweet managed the ballroom. During the big band era, the ballroom at Franklin Street featured the music of Benny Goodman, Lionel Hampton, Jimmy and Tommy Dorsey, Glenn Miller, Billie Holiday, Frank Sinatra, Duke Ellington, Harry James, and a host of others.

Oakland in the early 1930s had many a band stop here at Sweets and entertain all the citizens of our city. The bands would use the Oakland Auditorium at times, because the crowd was so big, for all to see and dance to the hot music. The big sounds were swing, jitterbug, jazz, rhythm and blues, and big band. Sweets dance hall had the atmosphere of a classy dancing spot. During the 1940s the big bands would draw crowds from all over Oakland. These were the swing years. A lot of Mexicans and Blacks would attend these dances with the big bands. This music was what the youth wanted. The intermingling of the people happened naturally. White, Mexican, Latino, and Black all got along. They were there for the fun and dance.

Music in the city was all across the neighborhood. People loved music and dance. West Oakland on Seventh Street down by the Point had some of the best nightclubs in town. At the Point we had two of the best and biggest blues clubs: Esther's Orbit Room and the Slim Jenkins Supper Club. These clubs catered to all the people. This was a Black neighborhood. These clubs also sold the best southern food. The restaurants were busy places. A lot of national touring acts stopped here. The music was hot and had a lot of rhythm.

During World War II, Kaiser Shipyards brought from the South a lot of manpower to work the shipyards, steel mills, and military bases. These people also brought to Oakland their food and new music sounds, namely the blues. Some of the musicians that stopped and played at Esther's Orbit and Slim Jenkins were people like B. B. King, Charles Brown, Jimmy McCracklin, Big Joe Turner, Teddy "Blues Master" Watson, Sugar Pie DeSanto, Saunders King, Ray Charles, Aretha Franklin, Ike and Tina Turner, and T-Bone Walker. These are only a few of the musicians that played West Oakland on Seventh Street. This thriving area of West Oakland was known as the Harlem of the West Coast. The big bands of blues musicians, with their ten players, most likely played Sweets Ballroom or the Oakland Auditorium. The shipyard workers and sailors would keep the local businesses busy. Seventh Street was hot.

The nightclubs on Friday nights and Saturday were full of people dancing to top musicians. The neighborhood in West Oakland also had pool halls, pawnshops, card rooms, theaters, cafés, bars, food markets. It was a self-sustaining community. The Latinos on Seventh Street during this period, 1930 to the 1960s, had their music. The old-timers had their country music that was played in the bars, social halls, and cafés. The recently arrived people in the 1930s liked the boleros, mariachis, rancheras, corridos, congas, rumbas, and polkas. The younger people liked the big band sounds of jazz, swing, and jitterbug. This young generation loved to dance to this music. Soon this new generation crossed the culture lines and left their neighborhood to dance and have fun. We had a large multicultural mix of young people enjoying music throughout the city of Oakland. Most people in the 1940s worked hard in the shipyards, foundries, Kaiser steel mills, and other factories during the war effort. The work was performed in ten to twelve hour shifts seven days a week. The workers were paid good money. Their time off gave them some opportunity to spend any extra money to have fun. So dancing was one outlet and a chance to socialize with others.

The vibrant music caught the people's mood. The Blacks had their version of sound and the Latinos had theirs. During the early 1940s the pachucos and pachucas had their version of dance and music. Zoot suiters and hepcats enjoyed the jitterbug, blues, and swing music being played at the clubs, dances, and events throughout the city. The zoot suiters and hepcats had their own style of dress. When anyone dressed that way they were perceived as juvenile delinquents. The racial prejudice and discrimination in Oakland made them a target for the police and Anglo citizens. Around 1943, Los Angeles had two to three days of Zoot Suit Riots involving the police, sailors, and military people. Oakland and San Jose youth also had their fight with the military and police. This was a big surprise for everyone in the city. Any Mexican youth that wore the pachuco style was the victim of this discrimination. This racial label left all the people with a bad taste. The dance halls in the 1940s began to turn away the Latino or Blacks from some of the dances. The managers hesitated to open up their dance halls to mixed groups. So they organized the kinds of music they would play to separate who came to dance. Sweets Ballroom would have the Blacks on Saturdays, the Latinos on Sundays. The Oakland Auditorium was bigger so they let all the races mix it up: Black, Latino, and Anglo.

Musical Melting Pot

The prewar youth, first generation Latino, were into swing, jitterbug, blues, jazz, and percussion beats. The tunes now playing at the dance halls and clubs were hot. This new generation did not want discrimination to stop them from attending dances or social functions in any part of Oakland. The police prejudice before the Los Angeles riots and after were challenged in the neighborhoods throughout the city. The hostile city and prejudice of the times were no longer okay. Music is what gets people of all cultures to mingle and enjoy the time.

Soon the 1940s music was changing. The new sounds were part of the youths' new choices; they listened and danced to the Afro-Caribbean music and percussion. I can remember the Puerto Ricans playing their style of music, the maracas, their folkloric guitar and the songs. The lyrics always expressed a lot of feeling. The new music with the new beats was played at social events, homes, bars, nightclubs, and dance halls. Oakland had a lot of dance halls besides Sweets: the Jenny Lind Hall, the Sands, the Ali Baba, the California Hotel, the Ninety-Eighth Avenue Puerto Rican Club, plus many nightclubs on Broadway downtown. Xavier Cugat was big in the East. When he brought his big band to the West Coast, he would play in Oakland's Sweets Ballroom. He was very popular. The singer Miguelito Valdes was part of this Latino music. He was a great singer. The public loved his songs. The Cuban music was also popular in Oakland and in San Francisco's Mission District. All the new sounds, Afro-Caribbean music and percussion, bolero, guaracha, mambo, rumba, foxtrot, blues and swing tunes were being played, with the American-Spanish lyrics being much hipper.

Oakland had a lot of musicians, as did San Francisco. These musicians played all around the Bay Area. The Latino population loved music and dance. I can remember how my brother Mario and his friends would prepare themselves on Saturday and Sunday to go dancing. The ritual required a dress suit, a crisp, lightly starched shirt with a classy tie, and shiny dress shoes. Hair was clean and combed many times to round out your appearance. These were the times to go listen to your favorite band and we had them: Merced Gallegos, Armando Peraza, Benny Velarde, Cal Tjader, Frank "Machito" Grillo, Willie Bobo, Mongo Santamaría, Tito Puente, Tito Rodriguez, Modesto Duran, Pérez Prado, Pete Escovedo, and Coke Escovedo.

Pete Escovedo and Family

The Escovedos in the 1950s had their own band, playing and starting in Oakland. I remember this West Oakland Escovedo family well, with their very talented musicians, from Pete's dad on down. My dad's shop, La Ideal Mexican Music Shop, was on Seventh Street. Pete Escovedo and his family lived on Market Street. As a young boy I knew Pete and Coke through the neighborhood. I remember going to see my first musical downtown at the Fox Oakland on a Sunday with Pete Escovedo and Mike Lozano. My kids all followed the Escovedo boys' careers. The Mexican and Latino people were looking up to these top musicians. Everyone was proud of Pete and Coke. During their start, Oakland was flourishing. The Latino West Oakland dance halls downtown on Broadway were going full swing on the weekends.

Pete grew up in West Oakland and attended McClymonds High School on Twelfth and Market. He knew the jazz and blues sounds that he heard coming out of the nightclubs down at the Point. He has played with many of the great bands: Santana, Carlos Federico, and others. He embraced jazz, Afro-Caribbean, and his percussion sounds in the Bay Area. My brother Mario, who heard lots of music while working with my dad at the Music Shop, always said the Escovedo boys were great. The boys had their own band. They called it Azteca. The band played the Bay Area for many years. They gave all the Latino people great music and pride in their success. Pete's daughter, Sheila E., started her career with her dad's band, Azteca. Pete is blessed how his children have followed in their grandfather and father's footsteps. The whole family is accomplished and has talent. They have had good guidance from Pete and Juanita, their mother who is a blessed mom.

I need to mention how the late 1940s through the 1960s was a new experience for all the people in West Oakland. Our generation did a lot. We had talent all around us. But I believe we made a decision during these times to focus on doing something to improve ourselves, and we did. We surpassed our dreams. What my brother Mario said about Pete and his brother Coke came true. They played lively music and gave an uplifting experience to the people listening to them. I remember Mom saying once that she knew that family back in the early 1920s in Pittsburg, California. She said that she worked with their mother; they are a good family. I know through Pete and myself, and the Cheveres family I speak of, that we have a special bond of family.

Western Music

Music in the 1940s through the 1970s had another new style. This kind of music was sometimes called hillbilly. As Latinos, our western music was the rancheras and mariachis. This other western music came to the Bay Area with the people from Oklahoma and Arkansas. We called them Okies or Arkies. This was neighborhood slang. In the 1930s people would call it hillbilly music. In later years it became part of the music known as country music. The sound would be on radio station KLX Oakland. The bands that played on the radio were popular, like Dude Martin, Stuart Hamblen, and Bob Wills and His Texas Playboys. San Pablo Avenue in Oakland was home to many a western bar all the way to Richmond. Dude Martin was a favorite in our area. He played at the large Sweets Ballroom, especially during the time before World War II and the buildup of the military bases, the shipyards, and the steel mills.

The Kaiser shipyards recruited thousands of men and women from the deep South and from mid-southern states such as Oklahoma, Arkansas, and Texas. The new arrivals brought their music with them. Working full-time as they did, they had money to spend on their favorite music places: San Pablo Avenue and new honky-tonks and large dance halls. Two large halls were Redmond Hall in Richmond and Maple Hall in San Pablo. The small clubs and bars also played western music. Some of these were John's Half Barrel, Crazy Joe's, Crabby Joe's Big Barn, and many other bars on San Pablo Avenue. The crowds were big during the war. The spirit was up all over and nightlife activities, both legal and illegal, kept people traveling up and down San Pablo Avenue. You could find gambling, offtrack betting, slots, prostitution, bars, dancing clubs, food places, and western music.

San Pablo Avenue also had a jazz club that opened in 1947. Lu Watters owned a club called Hambone Kelly's. This jazz club was popular in the early years after the war ended. Many nationally known jazz musicians stopped there to play.

The western music would include some blues, since some of the western musicians such as the great Hank Williams Senior recorded them. Two of his big hits were "Honky Tonk Blues" and "Lovesick Blues." The bars in the mid-1940s were busy places. Some of the most popular clubs were the Hotsy Totsy Club, Kona Club, Six Belles, Crabby Joe's Big Barn, and the Wagon Wheel. About 1950, the goodtime places began slowing down. Some places closed. Times had changed. The people were moving to new areas or even going home to Oklahoma, Arkansas, and Texas with their new money.

Then came along new stars with their music favorites, such as Johnny Cash, Kenny Rogers, and Willie Nelson, all big in movies and television, still playing the western sound. The music of all peoples in the prewar and 1940s through the late 1950s took a change. The Black music, the Latino music, and the western music all adjusted for new times. First the 78 rpm records gave way to the smaller 45 rpm records in time for the new rock and roll with Bill Haley and His Comets along with the big splash of Elvis Presley. The LPs, the cassette tapes, and the large 8-track stereo recording tapes gave people everywhere a chance to hear the great music we knew from West Oakland, and vice versa. Listening to live music for many became a real treat. Some dance halls and lounges and bars found it less expensive to hire disc jockeys who played from their own collections, first with tapes and then with compact discs (CDs). Now along comes the new computer downloads, handheld phones, and other electronic devices that people can carry with them. They can listen to their favorite songs without having to go down to the local dance halls or bars. I wonder if they know that they are missing out on the spirit and the fun of those lively days when the multicultural music of West Oakland could be heard all over the neighborhood and the dancing was to live music.

Family love of music through generations: Uncle Francisco (left, sitting) and Uncle Lupe (left, standing) with two other relatives; 1934, Oakland.

A photo of Pedro Infante signed with a special note in Spanish to Sarita, Ruben's mother.

Two boyhood friends, Pete Escovedo and Ruben Llamas, meet after many years.

Pete Escovedo, a Bay Area icon of Latino music.

Ceci Chevere interviews music icon Pete Escovedo on her 1990s cable TV program, *LTV*.

Ceci Chevere performing with Ruben Aponte on stage in San Francisco.

Courtesy of California Museum of Oakland

Xavier Cugat (left, with violin) and Guadalupe Carlos (right, in sport coat) at Sweets Ballroom Band Stand.

125

Mario Llamas dressed up for the Sunday *tardeada* at Sweets Ballroom, around 1950.

Poster advertising the Sunday *tardeadas* at Sweets Ballroom, 1932.

EIGHT

Special Musicians and Dancers

◆◆◆◆

Guadalupe Carlos: Promoter of the Sunday Tardeadas

Guadalupe Carlos was born in Mexico. He came to America around 1923 with his parents to escape the confusion remaining from the 1910 Mexican Revolution. He worked at Bethlehem Steel in Oakland. Sometime in the 1930s, Guadalupe began promoting dances at Sweets Ballroom. He was an entrepreneur with a vision. He wanted to put on dances and Mexican entertainment for his people. Sweets Ballroom at 1414 Franklin Street was one of the four ballrooms in Oakland managed by the brothers Eugene and William Sweet. At this time, discrimination against the Mexicans and the Blacks was all around and strong. The music of different cultural groups did not mix in the entertainment venues. The Mexicans, as did the Blacks, wanted to enjoy their entertainers and their kind of music and dance. Guadalupe had a vision of how the Mexicans of West Oakland could have their dances in the ballrooms that the Sweet brothers managed. Sweets Ballroom was a classy dancing spot with a great floor for dancing.

Guadalupe was a promoter. I can only assume that one of his many skills was being a good talker. As a promoter he had to have a business plan, a company, the ability to organize, plus financial backing to make his vision a reality. Whatever he had to do, his negotiations got him the classy ballroom for the *tardeadas*. This man had to be working hard to put these events together, especially considering that he had a full-time job at Bethlehem Steel.

As a kid, I remember shining shoes in my dad's barbershop. Guadalupe would come by La Ideal Music Shop to see Dad. I admired and respected this man, as he was always in a suit and looked well-dressed. He looked like a star. I could see that he was in a hurry. Now that I reflect back, I realize that he had reason to be taking care of business. The 1930s and the 1940s were the *Epoca de Oro*: The Golden Age of the Mexican entertainers. The Mexican films, stars, singers, and the bands were at the top of their entertainment skills. Guadalupe knew that the music culture of West Oakland was vibrant and that the Latinos loved to dance. Guadalupe had personality and was a good host. He enjoyed what he was doing. He was in the midst of Oakland's time of vibrant music on Seventh Street. We had the Black and Tan clubs like the cool Slim Jenkins and many more. In the 1940s we had many of the top big bands. While touring they would stop in Oakland. Sweets had the big dance floor to hold the dancers.

Guadalupe would bring from Mexico many of the big name stars, bands, and groups to fill his Sunday *tardeada*. He knew how to work hard and how to get things done. He knew how to work in the system of getting the stars across the border. He would even physically go help them do what was needed to bring them across, verifying their legitimate purpose for coming to the USA. At this time other promoters were out there, advertising their events. Also the 1940s and even into the 1950s were fun times. People were moving all over the city. The World War II effort made the shipyards a beehive. Steel mills, foundries, and the military bases were working 24/7. People worked hard, and in their time off they played hard. Guadalupe did a lot, working his job at the shipyards, raising a family, and promoting his vision of entertainment for his people.

Some of the Mexican stars and other Latino stars were people like Pedro Infante, Xavier Cugat, Jorge Negrete, Maria Victoria, Tin Tan, Fernando Soto, Toña la Negra, and many others. Guadalupe opened doors for many people, and he gave many local Latino musicians a place to play their music. In the late 1930s and into the 1940s, Merced Gallegos had his band playing at Sweets Ballroom. His house band played rancheras, danzones, boleros, guarachas, rumbas, foxtrots, Latino blues, and the mambo. He was a tough taskmaster; his musicians had to read music. Can you remember dancing swing, jitterbug, and blues with these great musicians? That was some time. His theme song for the band was "Santa (Bolero)," a song from the great icon, Agustín Lara.

Musicians that played at the *tardeadas* include Pérez Prado, Benny Velarde, Armando Peraza, Carlos Federico, Willie Vargas, Pete Escovedo, Coke Escovedo, Cal Tjader, Willie Bobo, Mongo Santamaría, Tito Puente, Machito, Tito Rodriguez, and the great Antoine "Fats" Domino. Something to note: twelve hundred people came to see the Mambo King, Pérez Prado, play his song "Cherry Pink and Apple Blossom White." This hit was at the top of the charts for twenty-six weeks. Pérez Prado visited La Ideal Music Shop on Seventh Street.

I write this about Guadalupe Carlos for all the people to understand the man behind the Sunday *tardeadas*. Guadalupe was also a linguist; he spoke six languages. His dances allowed people of all Oakland cultures to have fun in the classy dance ballroom. He knew that when all people get together, white, Black, and all Latinos, they relax and enjoy themselves with the great sounds. It has been my experience in talking with people about dancing and music events that music can be a great equalizer. Just mention the Sunday *tardeadas* at Sweets—everyone has that recurring memory of the great time they had. And the man behind these great moments was the promoter, Guadalupe Carlos from West Oakland—the entrepreneur with a vision.

From one of my interesting searches I found an article about the printer Guadalupe used. Tilghman Press printed the posters that Guadalupe himself designed. These posters were displayed in store windows and on street poles all over town. The Tilghman family was one of West Oakland's prominent Black families on Seventh Street. Guadalupe brought the stars into the area but he did business with the locals, assuring the success of the neighborhood as well as the success of his vision. Thus Guadalupe Carlos is remembered as a visionary whose promotions gave people fun times during and after the difficulties of World War II that affected everyone, especially the people of West Oakland.

Ceci Chevere: The Bay Area's Original Iconic Salsa Dancer

Ceci Chevere (born Cecelia Cheveres) began her love for Latino music as a young child. Her Puerto Rican roots gave her the spirit and passion for this Latino music. As a young child she heard the playing of folkloric guitar that Puerto Rican musicians played at social events. Her mom and dad had many great parties at home, and music was the highlight.

Ceci was born in Carpinteria, California, where some of her family members still live. Ceci's family moved to Oakland about 1930 or 1940 when West Oakland had a strong Puerto Rican and Mexican population. The two cultures mixed well in this neighborhood. Ceci married Mario Llamas, my older brother. Ceci's brother, Danny Cheveres, was my longtime childhood friend and my godson's father.

The Puerto Rican culture celebrates life and dance, and has this love of life's goodness. Ceci was a natural dancer and entertainer, and was passionate about salsa. Her mom would involve her in ethnic dancing and activities. In Santa Barbara she would perform in the Spanish fiestas dressed in ethnic costumes for the different folk dances. This was a learning experience at a young age. She grew up practicing and performing Mexican, Spanish, and Puerto Rican dances.

Ceci's parents moved to Oakland for a better life. Her dad was doing migrant work in Carpinteria, picking lemons. The pay for the orchard work was low, while the shipyards in Richmond, California, offered better pay. Ceci's parents spoke little English at this time; Spanish was their primary language. Both parents found work in the shipyard in Richmond, California. This humble beginning gave Ceci the strength to become the special person she was.

Her mom and dad saved money to buy a house on Myrtle Street. This financial improvement allowed the parents to give their children a good education for a better life. Her dad was the force behind his children getting a good education. The diversity of people in the neighborhood also gave Ceci an understanding of other cultures and their music. At the young age of fourteen, Ceci was introduced to the experience of ballroom dancing at Sweets. How did this happen at this early age? Her mom would send Ceci to chaperone her older sister Benita; this was a customary thing to do.

The Sunday *tardeadas* had some of the best Latino musicians and bands of this period. Ceci learned to dance to the rhythms of the bands of Pérez Prado, Tito Puente, Tito Rodriguez, Machito, Merced Gallegos, Lucho Gatica, Chico Ochoa, and Pete Escovedo. These Latin bands played the people's favorite rhythms. They had a good time at these Lupe Carlos Sunday *tardeadas*.

Dancing all around the Bay Area to boogie, mambo, Latin jazz, swing, and merengue, Ceci later taught salsa. Her life has always been full of the love of dancing. Her husband, my brother Mario, shared this love of music and dancing. Together on the dance floor they portrayed an excellence in dancing that everyone liked. Blessed with this musical skill, Ceci has had an influence on salsa music and dancing events.

Her talents have been many. She developed a dance and comedy character. The comedy act debuted at the Victoria Theater in San Francisco in 1991. She was a very popular entertainer in the Bay Area. In 1993 she hosted a local TV show called *LTV* (Latin Television). Ceci Chevere did interviews with VIPs of the salsa scene. She shared the salsa culture with the community. Many musicians, dancers, and singers appeared on her show. The people who appeared on the show include Willie Colon, Pete Escovedo,

Phil Escovedo, the Carl Perazzo dancers, Tito Puente, and herself, Cecelia Cheveres, with her stage name Ceci Chevere. In her words, she loved to dance and said, "I know I was born to dance!" She was excited about salsa dancing and her Puerto Rican roots. The inner child kept her going to dances. Her lifetime of musical experiences made her the remarkable person she was! Cecelia transitioned into the light on March 10, 2012.

Cecelia with her daughters and granddaughters.

Facing page: Emilio's mother (Ruben's grandmother) with family members in Mexico.

PART THREE
Looking Back

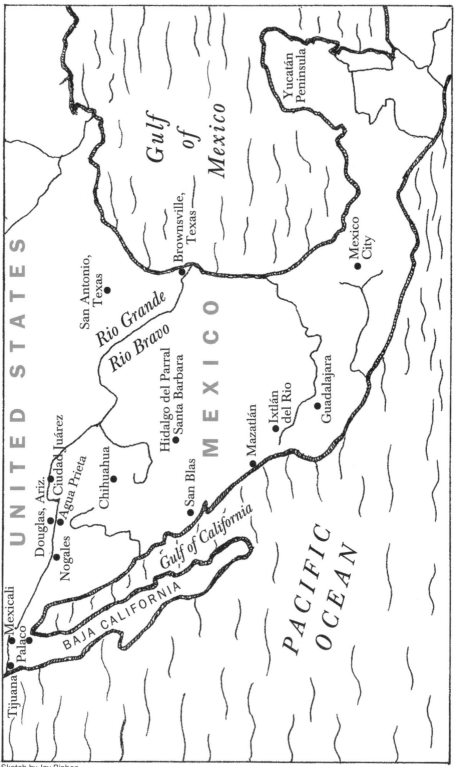

Sketch by Jay Bishop

NINE

California's Mexican Heritage

Indian Heritage

Native Americans originated from the people who, thousands of years ago, came from Asia to the North American continent by way of a dry land mass now covered by the Bering Sea. With the bounty of sea and soil, fish and nuts and berries, and mild climate, these Indian tribes, as they were called later by Americans, successfully survived for centuries before the earliest European explorers arrived by ship and sea along the California coast. The Ohlone Indian tribe living in the Oakland area had simple hunter and gatherer lives until Spain's control finally reached the Oakland area. Spain's control over Mexico started as early as the sixteenth century but took more than another century to reach the area of Oakland and the San Francisco Bay.

Early Settlements, Spanish Colonialism, and Mexican Rule

Early explorers sailed along what is now the Texas coast as far back as 1519. Spaniards moved into the interior of Mexico traveling both west and north. The first settlement was made at Ysleta, near El Paso, in 1682. By the early nineteenth century, Americans continued to move west into Texas, which at the time was part of

Mexico, as were other southwestern states. Mexico won its independence from Spain in 1821. California by that time had many Spanish and Mexican settlers as far north as Sonoma, California. Russians meanwhile had a few small settlements for fur traders in Alaska. They also established a fort at Fort Ross in northern California, north of Sonoma.

Spain's grand idea was to bring their way of life to their colonies and then develop pueblos with Spanish settlers. The Spanish Franciscan priests founded missions up and down Alta California, beginning in 1770s. Some of the earliest missions and pueblos in Southern California had moderate success with teaching the Indians language, rituals, gardening and agriculture, weaving, blacksmithing, wine pressing, and raising horses, cattle, sheep, and goats. The few missions that were paired with a presidio caused problems for the Indians. The soldiers could be rowdy or harsh in managing some Indians, even taking prisoners. The mission was supposed to be a place of learning and worship. So these missions were moved away from the presidios beginning with San Diego north. For example, the presidio for soldiers who guarded Mission Dolores in San Francisco was established several miles from the mission itself.

The Franciscan priest Father Lasuén founded Mission San José in 1797. This founding indirectly established the Oakland area, where overflow from the mission expanded with pueblos and ranchos. Getting this far north was an accomplishment; neither land nor sea routes were easy. Supply ships had a long dangerous voyage for getting supplies to Alta California, but the last treacherous stretch from San Diego to the San Francisco Bay Area was the worst. A few hearty trailbreakers, with the trust of the Indians, found a land route, but the trip was too unrealistic and difficult for colonists.

Mission Dolores was founded earlier than others because of its location near the San Francisco Bay. It was founded as Misión San Francisco de Asís in June 9, 1776. The name Mission Dolores comes from the name of a stream nearby called Arroyo de los

Dolores. This area has always had a strong population of Mexicans and Latinos. Notice that this Spanish and Mexican heritage predates the Declaration of Independence on the East Coast by nearly a month. San Rafael on the other side of the San Francisco Bay was founded many years later, in 1817.

The San Francisco Bay Area, including Oakland and San Jose, was far from the control of Spain, or even the Mexican government. All of Alta California was too remote for the Spanish government to govern or to even take notice of its conditions. The dream of the Spanish kings had been too broad. This lack of governmental control continued when the Mexican government took over control from Spain. Around the 1830s the missions were told to start the process to secularization. The mission fathers were told to dispose of their missions. Secularization meant releasing the missions from the control of the church. Because of the distance this also meant no government rule. Some Spanish soldiers settled with their families in a disciplined manner; others were less civilized.

Without either the military rule or the mission discipline, some of the released soldiers took advantage of the early Mexican settlers and of the Indians who were losing their homes again. By this time many of the Indians of this future Oakland area had either joined other tribal groups of their own heritage or had died of disease. With the extreme changes imposed on their way of life, few native dwellers were able to adapt. Some revolted and were killed. None could return to the simple sustainable life their people once knew. The changes in their way of life were severe, although some married the Spanish soldiers or settlers from Mexico, and blended in as those with Mexican heritage did. The native dwellers were never able to live within the culture they once had at this location.

In 1820, upon retiring from the military, Luis María Peralta was awarded a 44,800-acre land grant from the King of Spain called an empresario grant. This land grant, known as Rancho San Antonio, included most of present-day Alameda County. In

1842 *Don* Peralta divided this land grant among his four sons. Most of Oakland fell within these shares given to Antonio, Ignacio, Vicente, and José. This was prime land. Throughout the 1840s and 1850s American squatters laid legal claim to the land held by the Peralta family. The outcome to this land grab was the loss by the Peraltas of all of the Spanish land grant *Don* Peralta had received. With no government control the squatters had the upper hand, and the Peraltas lost their grants. Even the sons of a respected leader like *Don* Peralta had a broken legacy.

This is an example of what happened to most of the Spanish grants and to the Mexican people who held the deeds to their land. In 1821 Mexico became independent of Spanish rule. Mexico's territory included much of the western area of our country. In 1848 the United States' war with Mexico ended with the Treaty of Guadalupe Hidalgo, by which Mexico ceded its southwest to the United States. The Treaty of Guadalupe Hidalgo was signed in 1848 by Mexico and the United States. This is less than two hundred years ago. This agreement followed years of conflict, ending in the War of 1846–1848.

In 1821 empresario land grants were issued. These brought European American families to Texas, which was Mexican land. To get this grant, families had to (1) become Catholic and (2) pledge allegiance to Mexico. So some who were legal Mexicans were direct emigrants from Europe or the United States. These Mexicans had a Texas heritage, not a Spanish or true Mexican heritage. The 1836 Battle of the Alamo in Texas first was won by Mexicans and then retaken by Texans. By signing the treaty, Mexico ceded territory of not just Texas but also of California, New Mexico, Arizona, Utah, Nevada, and Colorado. This transfer of territory left some bad feelings, especially for those with Spanish or Mexican family heritage.

Although the War of 1846–1848 was not fought on California soil, Californians had problems of land ownership after the war. The 1851 California Land Act required grant holders to defend their title to their land when squatters claimed it. The

Land Commission held hearings in San Francisco, but were these commissioners able to speak, let alone understand, Spanish? The grants dealt with large acreage, used both for farming and for cattle grazing. More than half of these grants were decided in favor of the American or European American immigrants. Some of these people were caught in the middle because they themselves were "sold" the land from someone who had no land grant. The boundaries were large and not always well marked.

California became a territory under the military rule of America in spite of minor efforts at independence. When the courts examined the papers of the Mexican people who held title to the Spanish land grants, the courts usually sided with the Americans from the east. The courts were not about to let Californios or Mexicans keep their land grants, especially the grants that had been signed by the Spanish governors.

Gold Rush and Railroads

While Oakland's mild weather supported small farming, and the bay waters supplied a bounty of fish and other seafood, a new source of wealth lay hidden eastward across the central valley and up in the Sierra Nevada foothills. The native Indians knew of the gold in their rivers. But they did not realize how the white man would go crazy over this metal that one could not eat or burn for warmth. Soon gold seekers from all over the world started coming across the San Francisco Bay to get to the gold-filled mountains. In 1850 California became a member of the United States of America. Oakland had become one of the main staging areas between the San Francisco Bay and the many gold mines in the Sierra foothills. In 1852 the California legislature incorporated the town of Oakland. And the east-west railroads of the 1860s arrived soon after. Oakland would become the farthest west terminus for the continental rail lines.

Meanwhile the waterways along the Pacific Coast north to Oregon were busy with ships bringing goods and people to the booming Gold Rush areas. Although San Francisco remained the center for business and financial growth, Oakland served as a busy seaport, allowing direct movement from ships across the Central Valley to the golden hills of the El Dorado. People arrived by the hundreds through the busy seaports on both sides of the Bay.

Through the years, the weather of Oakland prompted a good number of San Francisco dwellers to leave the foggy hills of the city for the sunny coast of Oakland. My family and others lived in Victorian homes that were built by folks who moved from the chilly summers in San Francisco. The fire and earthquake of 1906 also caused other San Franciscans to move east . . . across the bay to Oakland.

Immigration North from Mexico

To the birds, the animals, the water, and the air, there is no boundary between Mexico and California. The boundary is an imaginary man-made line to indicate separation of nations and states. From a geographical perspective southern California, as well as Arizona and New Mexico, share many geographical features with Mexico. Before development of southern states, northern Mexico shared rivers with the USA. The water of many of these rivers naturally flows to the Gulf of Mexico and the Baja, when not redirected to American cities. The climate of both areas is comparable for miles before gradually changing to a more northern climate.

Some western areas of Mexico were settled by Europeans from other countries besides Spain. When Spain relinquished control of Mexico and the Mexican central government was formed, these western areas were still far from the influence of Mexican rule. Over time some farmers and dwellers rebelled against their Mexican presidents, or were incidentally caught in the rebellion of others against the harsh distant rule. The Revolutionary War of Mexico often carries the date of 1910. However it continued for years, at least in the western area of Mexico. Pancho Villa, a fugitive at a young age, spent many winters in the mild-weathered mountains of the area near Chihuahua, the home region of my grandparents.

Many people headed north, seeking peaceful areas to farm, to get good jobs, and to raise their families. Soon California's economy was thriving and needed hard-working people. A few towns along the border welcomed newcomers from Mexico into the United States of America. Mexicans came with their birth certificates in hand, and after a few hours at a border office they received their green card or other documentation, showing their birthplace and date of entry into the USA. California was a logical and reasonable destination for farmers, and for others who had long known how to find gold in their home areas of western Mexico.

The Repatriation Act of 1930 is a little-known shameful decision of the United States Government to deport people of Mexican heritage who entered the country legally and with documentation. This injustice was based on the false assumption that these legal residents who had been welcomed a decade earlier were taking jobs during the 1930s. Worse, those who were forced to return to Mexico were not allowed back into America, or became subject to restrictions on later visits. This meant that families were divided. Folks born in Mexico but who had legally entered California in the period 1900–1920, despite the documentation that they carried with them, were sent home. These were legal residents who had jobs and families. Their children, born in America, stayed and started families of their own. When grandparents later came back to see their children and grandchildren or needed help in old age, they were told to return to Mexico by some arbitrary deadline. In my family a few relatives of my mom voluntarily returned to their homeland. I visited them later with my brothers and sisters. I learned that they left America because of a simple desire to return to their homeland and the way of life they loved. Others were not so satisfied.

La Leyenda Negra (The Black Legend)

The Black Legend was a negative view of Hispanics; an attitude based on long-held biases of earlier centuries. As far back as the 1500s, Spain's enemies created a propagandized image of the people of Spain. Spain had become a very large over-reaching colonial empire. The Spanish people were viewed as cruel, corrupt, greedy, and barbarous. They were accused of slaughtering large numbers of Indians in the New World. The Dutch, English, French, and other European countries were jealous of all the discoveries by the rich Spanish nation that was receiving gold and silver from the New World. As the large colonial power it became, Spain was blamed by other Europeans for the ugly treatment and deaths of native dwellers in the Americas. Yet, in time, the pale-faced explorers and settlers of Anglo heritage themselves felt justified in taking over the land and wealth of the Mexican people and southern Americans. Many more northerly pale-faced Europeans held onto the mindset that Hispanics and darker-skinned people were their inferiors.

The negative opinion of the Black Legend encouraged newer settlers to seize Spanish lands. Spain lost its south and southeast colonies. This included Mexico, with its very large territory. In the mid-1800s, General Antonio López de Santa Anna was defeated by Anglo-Saxons who took over the Spanish colonies and realigned the borders. This land grab has not been forgotten by the Mexican people.

The Latino immigrants who gathered in the barbershop while I shined their shoes and my dad cut their hair discussed *La Leyenda Negra* with passion and resentment.

The older men also felt cheated by historians who neglected the contributions of Latinos in the development and success of America's beginnings. Little is told of how the Latinos helped early America in its Revolutionary War with England: how John Adams and Benjamin Franklin in Europe could not raise enough money for the war. George Washington and his troops were on the brink of dissolution without funding for their basic needs. The Cuban and Spanish women gave up their jewelry and raised millions to help the Americans fight for their independence. Men from the Latino countries fought in this war and died for the birth of this United States of America.

This is a sample of the Spanish contributions that we don't hear about. The Latino countries have helped in American wars, past and present. Our immigrant parents were happy that we have educated ourselves and not forgotten our own ancestral cultures. Yet our parents also insisted that we speak English at home and learn what we needed to participate in building the American economy and commerce.

Jesus (Jess) Llamas, Emilio Llamas, and their mother
Juana Santiago de Llamas, 1923.

TEN

Family History

◆•✦•◆

Emilio (August 5, 1908–August 26, 1967)

I would like to start with the journey of my parents from Mexico to the north. My father, Emilio Llamas, was born August 5, 1908, in Ixtlán del Río, Nayarit. Nayarit is a state in Mexico. Its border is the Pacific Ocean and inland next to Guadalajara. Ixtlán del Rio is also a major highway connection for the country's highway system. The railroad connections also are part of the town's importance. My dad was always talking of Mazatlán and San Blas. He mentioned the Pacific Ocean and the tropical fruits of the area. I believe he spent his teenage years in the two towns. Mazatlán and San Blas are old Spanish towns established in 1768 for their natural ports. The Spaniards did a lot of shipping to Spain of minerals, mainly silver and gold, in the late 1760s.

San Blas also became the base for Spanish expeditions to the Pacific Northwest and the missions of Alta California. Mazatlán is in the state of Sinaloa. It was founded in 1531. The Spaniards used this port heavily for its silver and gold mines. I remember my dad talking with Mr. Garcia, Anita's dad, about the climate and what fruits they grew in the area where he lived while growing up. Anita's dad was from Hawaii, and both dads agreed on the growing of the same tropical fruits, namely, mangos, papayas, and bananas. Mazatlán is also the hometown of Pedro Infante, one of the most popular actors and singers of the golden years of the Mexican cinema.

My dad, Emilio Llamas, came to the United States on September 6, 1923. He was fifteen at the time. Emilio's mother, Juana, and Jesus, Emilio's brother, came across the border at the same time. They crossed the border at Brownsville, Texas, with their documents in their hands. My father's mother's name was Juana Jimenez de Llamas. She also used the last name of Santiago. Dad's brother, Jesus I. Llamas, was my Uncle Jesus, whom we called Uncle Jess. He was six years old. Jesus was born in 1917 at Ixtlán del Rio, Nayarit, Mexico. Dad never said why they came to the United States.

My grandmother, Juana Jimenez de Llamas, had a brother already here in the United States. His name was Esperedeon Jimenez, and he was living somewhere in California. In old photographs of my grandmother and her brother, they are well-dressed with shoes that were current to the yearly styles. I never knew my grandmother. From talking with my mom, I believe she may have been what I would call a strong personality type. Mom once said she asked her mother-in-law to leave her home. Other than this, Mom never said much about my grandmother.

My dad did talk about living in Stockton, California, with his mother. He worked as a young man in the farm areas of Stockton. I would put his age about this time as sixteen or seventeen. Dad during this period attended barber school while doing farm work. I know he had to serve an apprenticeship period before he could be a master barber and open a shop. Stockton during this period of the late 1920s had a big population of Mexican people, and I know he cut their hair. Dad also was always looking ahead for ways to better himself. During this time he worked for an Italian barbershop owner in a neighborhood that had Mexican clients. I know that my dad worked there for some time and established himself with a good base of regular customers. I remember Dad was always patient with us as we grew up, and patient with customers. Dad was also strict with us as small kids, and I remember getting belted and spanked many a time.

In Stockton during 1920–1930, most Latinos and Spanish-speaking families usually established themselves in neighborhoods. They felt comfortable with their people. I believe Dad spent a few years working for the Italian barbershop, developing himself with clients. During this period he made friends with an Italian couple who helped him. Dad had a lot of respect for these people. They became my brother's godparents. Being asked to be a godparent during these years was a special mark of honor and respect. We always called these people *padrinos.*

Before meeting my mother, Dad was married in Stockton in July 1926, to a Mary Delgado from Argentina, South America. Mary and Dad knew each other before marrying, I am sure. After looking over old family pictures of these times, I believe that they may have had a son about two or three years old. During these times it was not uncommon for persons who married to have children prior to marriage. The old pictures show other people with my dad's family and this child. Dad was eighteen years old and Mary was sixteen years old when they married. The pictures do reveal that she had family in Stockton. I do believe that I have this older half-brother out there somewhere. Dad's wife Mary gave birth to a girl, Francisca Felipa Llamas, on October 4, 1927. This infant did not live long. She died November 17, 1927. The old pictures show both young parents grieving the loss of their baby girl. Francisca did not have a mortuary showing. Instead they had a showing at home. The old pictures taken at this time show a little boy who has a very true resemblance of our family. Francisca is buried in Oakland, California, with other relatives at St. Mary Cemetery. Dad and Mary after this event were still in Stockton or Oakland. Mary Delgado, Dad's wife, died February 14, 1930, of tuberculosis. She died in Stockton and is buried in St. Mary Cemetery, Oakland. I believe Dad had moved to Oakland where he lived and where he died, many years later.

When Anita and I first were married, she worked at Milens Jewelers on Twelfth and Washington. This street was the center of downtown Oakland after the war. One of her customers was talking with her, and somehow the customer and Anita talked about her marrying one of the Llamas boys. The lady asked, "Are you married to the oldest boy?" Anita said, "No, not Mario but Ruben." Anita mentioned that Eva Llamas was the oldest in this family. The lady said, "I know this family where there is an older son before Eva or Mario." She was insistent. This incident is a clue to the pictures of the two- or three-year-old boy in the pictures with my dad and Mary. I believe that the story of this older son is true. When I approached my mom she was very offended. She said that Anita's information was not true. We never resolved this issue.

In the late 1920s Dad moved to Oakland, which at that time had a large Mexican population. He opened his own barbershop on Seventh Street. During the years Dad added other things to sell. The shop's biggest sellers were the 78 rpm records, jewelry, huaraches, RCA and Zenith radios, record players within cabinets, refrigerators, and jewelry watch repairs. In the 1930s Seventh Street was a busy place from Broadway to the Oakland Mole, or Point, as we called it. Oakland had a strong presence of Latinos living through out West Oakland. Both sides of Seventh Street, going west to east, had businesses on each side plus many light industries and factory-style shops. During the years into the 1950s, families were the strength of this neighborhood. Dad bought the property his shop was on and we lived above. In the 1930s West Oakland was a thriving neighborhood, a diverse area to live in. One of the big things I remember is an extensive streetcar system that connected you to intercity rail lines and to the ferry lines.

Dad's shop did well during these times. The barbershop was busy. The weekends were good; all the men wanted to look their best for the Sunday dances. One thing about a barbershop, it was always a place to hang out. The local men would come in to talk, gossip, drink, and gamble, which they liked to do; gambling was big in Oakland in the 1930s. The music shop was also a busy place. My brother Mario ran that for Dad. Mario was a natural. He had charm, charisma, for people. The bar owners liked to deal with him. He sold a lot of records. He had a lot of musical friends that would come by to see him and to listen to the new hits. I remember riding with Mario in his old 1930s four-door Ford sedan to go to practice sessions of some of his musical friends. Mario had a good ear for music. He developed this at a young age. Mario was an excellent dancer. I remember Mario hooking up a speaker system on the front part of the music shop's building so people outside walking by could hear the new music hits.

In the mid 1930s my Uncle Jess also became a barber and worked with his brother Emilio, my dad. During this period someone, I assume, taught my uncle the watch repair business. I know he knew the repair business and the jewelry part of it. I can only say that Dad and Uncle Jess advanced themselves to improve their life and families. In the early 1930s Dad's mom was alive and living in West Oakland close to both her sons, Emilio and Jesus. In these times families lived together and took in boarders. Rent was cheap. The Depression was still affecting the economy of this country and neighborhoods.

My dad had become a citizen of the United States of America on August 27, 1945. This was a happy event, and he was very proud of this accomplishment. It was also the end of World War II. So these good things helped him with his sadness over losing his mother, Juana, who died September 27, 1941. So for a while things were very good for him. Then in the late 1940s and part of the early 1950s Dad had a difficult time.

In this time period my Uncle Jess opened his own barbershop, La Joyería y Relojería Mexicana. My dad was happy to see his brother open his own shop and improve his position in the neighborhood. Jess was a personable man. He knew a lot of people. His shop was near Washington Street. My uncle, I can remember, seemed to always be a fun person. It was fun to see him. My uncle also worked with the nearby air bases to repair the dials of the military planes during this wartime. Uncle Jess was married to my Aunt Katie. They had four kids: Ronald, Juanita, Jess, and Richard Llamas.

Jess and Katie bought a house in East Oakland on Fourteenth Avenue near Oakland High School. They had some problems in their marriage. I can recall Mom saying to me that Uncle Jess would be taken to a ranch somewhere in the valley to get some rest. We visited this ranch in the summer. I saw my uncle there and everything looked well for him. On August 8, 1949, my Uncle Jess hung himself with a clothesline in the back room of his shop. His wife, Katie, discovered him. He and his wife were having domestic difficulties at this time and had reconciled after a separation. He left her a note saying he was sorry for what he was doing and wrote, "I always loved you in my own way."

This incident had a strong impact on our family. My dad took his brother's death very hard. My Uncle Lupe, the cousin of my dad and Jess, also was involved with whatever led up to my Uncle Jess's death. One thing I do remember vividly was visiting a ranch in Acampo outside of Lodi with people Dad knew, the Salcidos. My Uncle Jesus was there with all his children. My dad said to keep away from my Aunt Katie. I believe they could have been having marriage problems and Uncle Jesus had to have his time to think. After the death my dad again said we needed to avoid Aunt Katie. I never understood what that meant. I would see her in the neighborhood and would always respect her and say hello. To me she was still my uncle's wife, and I never forgot it.

Now I remember the dinners at her and Uncle Jess's big house on Sixth Street, when I was a young boy. The house had a large garage. It looked like they parked trucks on the bottom floor. Uncle Jess and his family lived upstairs. The dinners were always on Sundays. My dad would take us all to the house, plus other family would be there. Aunt Katie was as tall as my Uncle Jess. She always was dressed well and had good posture. I remember her dark hair with her light skin. She was an attractive lady. I know she was a good lady. I still can remember going to her café on Seventh Street and seeing her in her working smock. Katie's full name was Katherine M. Llamas.

After my Uncle Jess's death my father, through his emotional hurt, did not want us to visit my Aunt Katie. As time passed on I can remember talking with my brother Mario. He always said to ignore what happened and that Aunt Katie was a strong lady. When my brother Mario died, she came to his burial and I was very appreciative of her doing that. It was like saying the past is over with. My deepest regret is that I should have visited her or called her more often. My mother, I know, had kept in touch with Katie so I was happy for that. Mario was right. She was a strong lady.

I met up with Aunt Katie's kids, my cousins, in 2010, after fifty-one years: Ronnie, Juanita, Jesse, and Richard. We Llamas are now close because I love them so much, and we spend time together when we can. I believe that family never disappears. We still have something in our deepest part of us that we bring back to enjoy each other like it was yesterday. Parents sometimes make mistakes that are filled with emotion and not logic. So now we will move on and review the hidden agendas and obligations that kept us apart.

Our neighborhood was changing as people were moving away to the outskirts. I can remember now that Dad did change when his brother died by hanging. I can't say how, but something was different. This kind of event is one of the most difficult a family can face. As a young person I did not understand enough and perhaps did not give him some companionship that would have helped him. Typically he let me go about my busy growing years. He was a good man challenged with the losses life sometimes gives us.

I will bring up now Pedro Infante. As I said in the music section, Pedro was a Mexican singer and film star in this time of the 1940s and '50s. When he became a star, promoters would bring him to Oakland for their events. Dad and Pedro were good friends. Both of them had history in Mazatlán. Pedro would come to see my dad, and they would talk about the music business, Pedro's singing, and what songs were new. When Pedro Infante died in 1957, my dad lost a good longtime friend. The list of Dad's great losses was getting too long. These special deaths—his first wife, a baby daughter, his mother and his brother, and now his dear friend, Pedro—changed him. Then came a change that was the death knell of West Oakland as we knew it.

The city had announced the building of the Nimitz Freeway right through West Oakland. The music business for Dad's shop had been changing. The moving out of the Latino population, the ending of the Bracero Program, all of these things had an impact. The new sounds in Latino music caught the ear of the young people. This hurt Dad's music business. The older people still enjoyed the older ranchera music of the mariachi, but the younger people were into the new music with the new size of records, so the 45s started to replace the 78s.

Jazz was also being embraced by the Mexican American teen generation, and by the fans of Afro-Caribbean music in the Bay Area. During the 1950s to 1960s a lot of great musicians were playing in San Francisco and Oakland. The market for the new music by of the Latino people had broadened. My dad's shop somehow continued through the 1950s, with more difficult times coming in the 1960s. I myself in 1958 went to work for PayLess Drug Stores and could not help my dad much in the shop. Mario had gotten married and also could not help Dad much. Dad had to depend on my sister Eva and himself. This was a difficult time for him and his shop. On top of this difficulty, he became ill with diabetes.

The decline of the neighborhood continued. After the war more newcomers wanted to live in Fremont, Walnut Creek, Concord, and where the new homes were being built. The old homes in West Oakland were decaying with no upkeep. The area was considered blighted and in need of help. The city was ready to put in freeways and tear down all they could in West Oakland. Lower Seventh Street and the Mole for Southern Pacific trains were now closed down. The industrial base was closed. Small business storefronts closed. The area was in a big slump. My dad always said if you opened a shop on your own property you could succeed. And this did prove right for him for many years.

In the 1960s Dad got real sick. He lost his eyesight. His diabetes got worse. He had a stroke and died August 26th, 1967. My mom closed the shop in the late sixties. The city bought her property, and she moved to East Oakland behind St. Elizabeth High School with my sister Eva. Dad had a good life, and he did his best with his shop. I know I learned from him that if you work hard and each day look to improve yourself, you will succeed.

Sara Garcia (March 16, 1911–November 30, 1990)

My mom was born Sara Garcia in Santa Barbara, Chihuahua, Mexico, on March 16, 1911. Her father's name was Augustin Garcia and her mother was Juana Soto de Garcia (Juana Florea de Garcia).

The state of Chihuahua, Santa Barbara, was a colony of Spain, the furthest from Mexico City. It became an important stop for people moving north. Santa Barbara was a mining region, with agricultural and stock ranching. People in this area experienced a lot of Indian uprisings, from Apache, Comanches, Yaqui, and other indigenous people. Chihuahua was largely colonized in the seventeenth, eighteenth, and nineteenth centuries. Entrepreneurs were attracted to this northern area because of gold and other precious metals. The area developed with haciendas and ranchos springing up. Thus a distinct regional economy that was founded on mining, livestock, and agriculture quickly developed on the frontier. The settlers on the Chihuahuan frontier were always alert and armed to fight off the potential rebels. Not the elite, the church, nor the Spanish government was able to secure dominance on this frontier compared to what they exercised in the rest of their society. These people were constantly at war – Indian wars – and were a hardy group.

My grandfather, Augustin Garcia, born sometime between 1876 and 1885, was probably in Chihuahua all his life. His parents

raised him in this land of war (*tierra de guerra*). So probably, as with ·
most people of this time, he grew up and lived with strict codes
of honor. They had no law enforcement officials to keep order. I
can imagine his outlook on life in this time. Being shaped in this
environment, he must have gained a cultured way of life. During
the 1880s to the 1920s, this district of Chihuahua, especially Santa
Barbara and Parral, had to develop many of its own unwritten
rules. Cultural values were the primary element forming the
working class in the northern Mexican mining region. The rich
society with its elite classes wanted to improve the working classes
to be responsible and better-skilled workers in a decent society.

Augustin Garcia was probably raised on a ranch in Parral. I
believe that Augustin worked the gold mines in the Santa Barbara and Parral area. He had the knowledge to search the ter-
rain for gold and to recognize if any other metals of value were
there. You have to remember, in the 1800s mines were worked
by hand with the simplest tools of the day. Most decisions about
where to dig had to come from experienced miners. Augustin
also must have had his hands in agriculture, growing crops. Mom
always said her dad was a good farmer. Augustin married my
grandmother, Juana, when she was fifteen. He had seen Juana in
church. He asked her parents for permission to marry her. They
had seven children: two boys and five girls: Tila (born 1902),
Francisco "Pancho" (1906), Arcadia (1907), Augustin (1908), who
died as a child, Martha (1910), Sara (1912), and Enriquetta (1914).

Augustin during this time was caring for a large family. To feed
his family he had to be farming, most likely in Parral or Santa
Barbara. He raised corn, squash, chickens, pigs, and horses to
sell locally. My grandfather had to be in this area at least twenty
years. During these times you needed help to work a farm and a
mine. An Indian man from the local area, who could be given
a place to live for himself and his family, could provide cheap
labor. Mom said that the Yaqui Indians who were related to the
Apache tribe worked on the farm. My grandfather knew where

there was a black outcropping. This indicated that gold was near. He would go there and take gold and live on it for a while. This is how he was able to improve his ranch and succeed.

Mom said many times that life on the ranch was good. They had all the food they needed to survive. The nearby city of Parral was also a station for Spanish settlers going north to California, Colorado, New Mexico, and Arizona. This city was known to be the most European in all Mexico. Parral had a strong Spanish and French presence, because the French along with the Spanish founded Parral. Parral is also known for its beef dishes and *dulce de leche* candy.

Unrest was always present for all the people: the farmers, rancheros, miners, and large landowners. Somewhere in the early 1900s my grandfather must have known Pancho Villa. Mom said Augustin's ranch grew crops but that he also grew crops on Pancho Villa's ranch. The deal was to grow crops and receive half of what had been grown on Villa's ranch. During this same time frame, my grandmother, Juana Soto de Garcia, was the cook for the Villa family on the Villa ranch. I try to put myself in this time period to understand how could both my grandparents get close to the Villa family. If you look back to see how people lived and communicated with each other, you see that they had a close relationship with other ranching people.

In 1910 the cloud of revolution was over all the territory of Chihuahua. I once asked my mom why did they leave. She said her father had lost his farm and had to move closer to town. I believe this was the start of working with the Villa family to sustain himself and his family. They must have spent some time here in Parral. In the years leading up to the Revolution of 1910, it must have been a dangerous place to live. With Augustin Garcia's family now much larger, plus the constant pressure of war around them, he probably had to make yet another change. He could see it coming. One interesting thing that did happen at the time of the start of war is that my Uncle Pancho, the oldest Garcia son, was taken by Villa's army to fight with them. My grandfather had Yaqui Indians go get my uncle back, and they did. Mom said this was about the time they left Chihuahua as a whole family.

Mom said they traveled to Sonora from Chihuahua by cart and horse. This trip was hard. They saw dead corpses hanging from trees. The *Villistas's* victims were always put on display to frighten the people. Uncle Pancho knew someone in the military. They were able to ride the train north by riding on top of the train. Their destination was Douglas, Arizona. My grandfather bought a lot and started to build a house. But he loved the mountains and was looking for a vein of gold. He found a big red house up on a hill. It was even near a river. The railroad tracks were close by also. My grandfather was a good farmer who knew the land and how to farm it. But he still knew how to find gold, even at the new location. Augustin would take Uncle Donato to the gold site but never showed him how to find it.

Augustin must have found something of value because he was able to move his family to the red house. But it was not enough to match the struggle to raise his family. Life was using up all his gains. And his years would be cut short by a fever. The farming he started here succeeded, but here in the red house all the family became ill. Augustin was hit the hardest by this illness. The fever took its toll. The doctor told Augustin not to ride his horse. But he wanted to see the crops. Not accepting how ill he was, he rode out anyway. My grandfather Augustin, patriarch of this Garcia family, fell off his horse and died.

The family now joined together to make a decision to cross the border into the USA. They did not all move to the United States at the same time. Most of them came in 1923. But Aunt Tila and Aunt Enriquetta came across earlier, around 1918. They moved into Douglas, Arizona. My Aunt Tila married Donato in Douglas. Uncle Donato had worked in the mines and on the railroad. He also made moonshine and sold it in Douglas, Arizona. He did time in prison for this bootlegging. The family did make one more move, this time to California. My grandmother, Juana Soto, moved to Oakland, California; Tila along with Donato moved to Fresno; Francisco (Pancho), Sara, Martha, and Enriquetta eventually came north to Oakland.

Before my mom, Sara, came to Oakland, she had lived in Pittsburg, California, working in the cannery there. She said she worked with a friend of hers in the cannery, a Mrs. Escovedo. Mrs. Escovedo also moved to Oakland. Her sons were among the talented musicians mentioned in the chapter about music and dance in West Oakland. By this time it was around 1930. My dad was a widower who was a shop owner with a barbershop, a music shop, and jewelry shop all in one location. Mom met and married my dad, and a new life started for both of them. They were married November 16, 1930, in California.

My mom, Sara Garcia, daughter of Augustin and Juana, and my dad, Emilio Llamas, had six children: Eva, Mario, me, George, Victor, and Juanita; four boys and two girls. We lived on Seventh Street in Oakland above my dad's shop. The old house had three floors: the top floor included the main kitchen area plus three bedrooms. The second floor was about the same. The old Victorian houses were built around the turn of the century, and by 1930 they needed outside work. During the late 1930s and 1940s Mom enjoyed cooking and having people over on Sundays. Mom was at her best as a person during these times. She was a believer in keeping us kids clean. During the late 1940s and early 1950s life in the area was changing. Dad was also becoming ill due to his diabetes. Mom in the mid 1950s wanted to move out of West Oakland, so we did. We moved to a corner house in San Lorenzo. This house was nice. It was larger than the old house on Seventh Street. Dad had to drive in to the shop on Seventh Street.

Dad was becoming ill, and the drive was hard for him. Mom sold the house in San Lorenzo, and they moved back to Seventh Street. The freeway would soon force her out of her Seventh Street house. Mom loved to shop at Swan's Market and the Housewives market. The old people at the different fruit stands, meat stands, and fish stands knew her. This market was where all people of

different cultures shopped. It was multicultural before any ter-
minology about different people of different cultures was used.
People just shopped there, mingling together naturally.

Living on Seventh Street in the 1960s was difficult for Mom.
Dad was home, but by now blinded by his illness. Then he had a
stroke. Mom had a lot of work put on her. Dad died in 1967. Then
Mom had to move to East Oakland behind St. Elizabeth High
School. The house behind the high school was about one block
west of Thirty-Fifth Avenue on a corner. Mom's house was a stopping place for my three brothers, Mario, George, and Victor. In
those days everyone was drinking, beer and liquor. My brothers
drank excessively, and it started to take its toll. Mom, being the
good mother that she was, allowed them to shower, and of course,
she fed them. I did not want her to allow this so much. But she
did it anyway. She could not turn them away. This is how she was.

Mom liked the neighborhood, the nearby church, and having
her grandchildren living by her. The times I visited her or stayed
in later years when Anita and I had the flower shop, I enjoyed
being with her. Mom was a great lady. I now wish I had asked
her more questions about the past. I believe her early life was
hard on her. Being poor in Mexico was no fun. I had asked many
times about what race of people we were. She said that she was
Mexican, Spanish, French, heavy on the Spanish. She said my
dad, Emilio, was Mexican. Mom did have an unusual trait. She
had this thing about not getting dark. She took good care of her
skin. Mom died November 30th, 1990, of colon cancer.

After Mom's death, I had to clean out her house. I was surprised
to find an old black box with black envelopes. In these envelopes I
found pictures of my dad's first wife and child. The baby was in a
white coffin for viewing, with my dad and his wife standing next
to it. In researching this pictured event, I questioned my older
brother Mario. His answer was, "Yes. Dad had been married
before marrying our mom, and his family had died. Dad married
Mom and they started a new life in the 1930s."

I learned from Mom the importance of being a person of honor, respect, and integrity, and of having the hope to succeed. Mom always kept pushing ahead, not giving up. She always tried her best. She lived a good life. She was a private person. The example and what I learned from both my parents gave me a solid foundation for my life, valuing my family through good times and difficult times, and using good hard work to succeed.

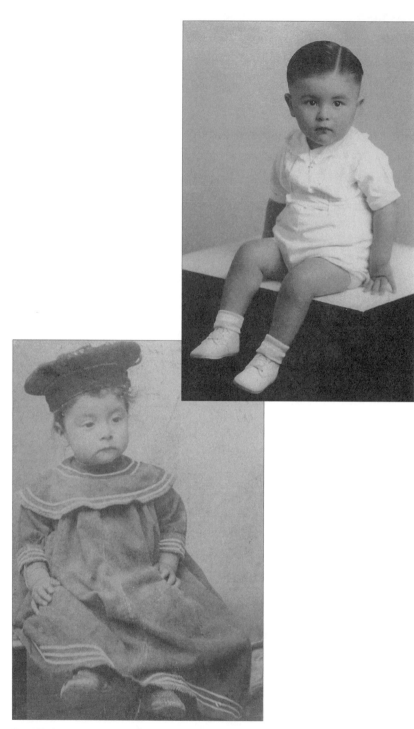

Top: Ruben Llamas as a toddler in Oakland.
Bottom: Emilio Llamas as a toddler in Mexico.

A special Italian couple were family friends. Ruben's parents referred to them as *padrinos*. They were highly respected and had a ranch in Brentwood with large orchards.

Juana Santiago de Llamas, her son Emilio, and her son's wife Mary with their deceased baby, 1927.

Emilio Llamas
and Sara Soto de
Garcia.

The wedding picture of Emilio Llamas and his second wife, Sara.

ELEVEN

Special Relatives and Friends

———◆•❧•◆———

Martha Soto Garcia (January 30, 1910–May 28, 2006)

My aunt Martha Becerra was a special lady to me. She is my mother's sister and my godmother. Martha was born in the Parral, Chihuahua, area in 1910. She lived on the ranch with her mom, dad, brother, and sisters. Martha had an interesting life as a young girl, but there was a lot of sadness in it. When she was about seven or eight years old, Martha's mother, Juana, my grandmother, allowed Martha to live with a family in Douglas, Arizona, before her birth family moved to Arizona. Her godmother, a woman named Maria Trueba, took Martha in to give her a better life and to help her get an education. Her godmother was good to her. Martha always missed her own mom and family. She shed many tears throughout her life for the loss of their presence in her life as a young girl. She once, as a young lady, did go back to see her family in Parral or Santa Barbara, Chihuahua. She said the only travel was by train, and it was a dangerous journey. She made it to her family's red house on a hill. When she arrived all the family were sick. She could not stay long.

In my visits with my Aunt Martha through the years, she once told me a story about herself and the family that I found interesting.

In Mexico City, on June 24, 1930, she married a military doctor, Jose L. Vela, from a wealthy family. He was also a pilot. She was married to him for five years. They never had children, which she thought was her fault. Martha lived a privileged life. However, the doctor was an alcoholic and Martha's life was difficult in spite of the wealth. The doctor was shot and killed.

Martha stayed with the Vela family for a while. They helped her get over the emotional death of her husband. Martha left Mexico, but she remained close to the Vela family throughout her life. My Aunt Martha, my godmother, was a lady. She never complained. She moved on with her life. I am glad she told me this story. I know the past gave her the strength to be such a special person.

Martha later joined her sister Sara, my mother, in Oakland, California. My mother introduced her to Eugene Becerra. Mom was impressed with Eugene. He hung his clean wash on the clothesline very neatly. Mom said he would be a good catch for Martha. Martha and Eugene married. He was a good man. My aunt had three girls and two boys. He worked for the Southern Pacific Railroad for forty-five years at the Oakland Mole. They were married for over fifty years. Later in life, they took a trip to Mexico and visited the Vela family. The Vela family welcomed Martha and Eugene with open arms.

I will never forget my Aunt Martha. She loved her family and she loved life. She took good care of her family. I love her. She to me was one of the stronger Garcia women in this family.

Eva Llamas (February 17, 1932–September 3, 1986)

My sister Eva was born February 17, 1932, in Oakland. Eva was the firstborn in our family. My sister was a good daughter. She loved her parents and was very close to them. I always admired this devotion that she showed to them and to us as her brothers. I always think of her in a special way.

Eva attended St. Mary's School on Seventh Street. She graduated and then attended Holy Names High School by Lake Merritt, which was later moved. Eva helped my dad in the shop during her growing up. The shop was a busy place in the late 1940s. The shop sold a lot of 78 rpm records of the many top Mexican stars. Eva had a very light complexion and light hair. She did not look Mexican. Mom would say Eva took to her Spanish side. I would always see my sister as being able to mix well with her white schoolgirl friends. She blended in well. She was lucky she grew up during the Second World War. This was an interesting time: 1940–1945 in West Oakland. With the military bases, shipyards and the steel mills, the city was busy.

Eva was a polite girl, though a little shy. She knew her place in this time. As a girl she was a respectable person. My sister did not have the good health that most of us boys had. I always remember Mom taking her to the doctors on Pill Hill for various illnesses. She continued to have stomach problems throughout her life. She lived at home on Seventh Street with my mom and dad. This arrangement was good for her. She had learned from working in other stores that she preferred working at our La Ideal Music Shop. During the time she was home, Mom and Dad needed her help because their health was not good. Eva in the 1950s had a very serious event happen to her. She was a victim of date rape. This emotional event plus her health problems left her very mistrusting of men. I never knew of this tragedy that affected her life until the late 1970s. Mom and Dad never mentioned it. They should have said something to me.

Eva continued taking care of Mom and Dad. She put them first, herself never marrying. After Dad died in 1967, Eva took care of Mom with her colon cancer. The care she gave Mom helped her to live a good life. In fact, Eva died from a rupture in her stomach before Mom died in 1990. I think of her as my sister that knew her responsibility to her parents, and I remember with thanks the love she gave to her brothers and sisters while never faulting any of us.

Mario Llamas (August 15, 1933–September 24, 1998)

Throughout this book I have mentioned my older brother, Mario, because he was a large presence for me from childhood on. Here

I would like to tell you how I remember him. He was the oldest
of the boys in our family. Mario helped Dad in the shop starting
about age ten or eleven years old. He was an especially big help
to Dad during the early period of World War II. I am sure he
absorbed the active lifestyle on Seventh Street.

In 1946 and 1947 he would go to Sweets Ballroom for the Sunday *tardeadas* to sell Mexican song books of the performers. My
brother was young when he was attending the Oakland music
and dance scene. He had already developed a good ear for music.
Many of the high-caliber musicians of the late 1940s and early
1950s would come to the shop to see him and listen to the new
Latino hits. The shop sold sheet music, and Mario was the person
who always kept the sheet music updated. He had a good way
with people. They respected him and his knowledge of music.
His interest in music would take him all over the Bay Area. He
would attend the events of the musicians of the early 1950s and
'60s. I learned from him the importance of dressing up to attend
these dance events. To him, dressing in a classy way was part of
this music scene. He always had a finished-looking suit and all
the accessories to match.

Mario attracted a small core of good friends, such as Gene
Flores, Gene Tropiano, Dick Stratman, Al Guerrero, and many
others. In the early 1950s the dances with their great music were
one kind of event that Mario and his friends attended on a regular
basis. The guys would work during the week, looking forward
to socializing and meeting new people at the events of the weekend. Mario knew everyone at Sweets Ballroom, so the Sunday
tardeadas were the usual for Sunday afternoon. They had a great
male camaraderie of finding new and exciting places to go. They
all had a lot of charisma and attracted many friends at any event
they attended.

Music was one of the many activities they enjoyed at the local
dance halls. New music could be found on the radio; then they
would find out where it might be played. Sometimes they would
follow the bands. Radio stations had many hosts to present the

music. Jumpin' George Oxford, Oakland's KWBR Swingin' Deacon, is an example. They kept us in music all day long: Fats Domino, Little Richard, Chuck Berry, Elvis, rhythm and blues groups, and the new English bands.

About 1951, Dad took Mario, Gene Flores, Gene Tropiano, and Dick Stratman to Tijuana and Ensenada. Dad would go on buying trips to Tijuana for gold jewelry and many other goods. I did go with Mario and Dad on such a trip, but this trip Dad took Mario and his close friends. They had a great time in Tijuana. They attended a bullfight, nightclubs, and other fun places. Dad also took them to Ensenada. This was a big plus. We had a young man from that area live with us in Oakland for a while, and his parents became good friends with Dad. Servando came across the border in 1950. We took him in. Mom and Dad treated him like the rest of us. Ensenada was his home. His family owned a hardware store, and his wife's family owned a French restaurant on the main highway across from the clean, natural coast beach. Ensenada in the early 1930s had been a small fishing port with a prime beach. Today it's a number one tourist attraction in Baja, Mexico. This was an exciting and interesting place for my brother and friends to visit.

I remember Mario buying his first car. It was a 1930s Model A, a maroon four-door sedan. This car kept Mario occupied daily. You could tear down the engine and put it together yourself, and that is what he did. He always parked it in the street in front of the shop, as we had no garage. He eventually sold this Model A and bought a loaded black 1934 Ford three-window coupe that had a leopard interior with chrome window trim. The car was raked, with smaller wheels in front, and had a 350 engine and a lot of power. He once took me out on a Sunday before the Nimitz Freeway opened up. He got on the construction site at the foot of Oak Street. He opened the car up and we roared down the freeway toward East Oakland with the pedal to the metal. We almost missed the Twenty-Third Avenue turnoff into Jingletown. I will never forget this moment with my brother, giving me this ride in the 1934 Ford coupe. When Mario was drafted into the army he sold the three-window Ford, and I still to this day wish I had this Ford coupe.

Through all his years, Mario created a huge record collection of many Latino artists, swing, R & B, jazz, percussion, and the best of the big bands. We were not surprised when Mario married Cecelia Cheveres. Mario with his great love and knowledge of the lively music, and Ceci with her love of dancing, were a great match. Cecelia and Mario would attend house parties, social events, and dance events at Sweets Ballroom, the Jenny Lind, or in San Francisco. They took over the dance floor and excited the crowd with their dance style. Their perfect timing as a dancing couple was mesmerizing. They added fun for everybody at the dance hall.

Mario and Ceci had two children, Mario Jr. and Michelle Llamas. The exciting times with the music often included lots of drinking. This gradually took its toll. Mario and Ceci separated, and Mario let his life and future slip away. Alcoholism took over his life, and he would not accept any advice to treat his disease and correct his behavior. He hurt himself very seriously and had brain damage. During this time he had to be committed to a convalescent home in Hayward. All the years I visited him he never complained of his situation. All the family, the Llamas, the Cheveres, and his good friend Al Guerrero helped in trying to make his situation easier. Mario made his decision and would not change. He lived with his choice, never complaining. He died in Hayward in 1998. He was buried in Oakland near our father and mother.

George Llamas

My brother George was born in Oakland in February 1940. As a young boy George was always active. He was good with people, always willing to help out his friends. George had a light complexion like our sister, Eva, who was the oldest in our family. Of all the boys, George was most obedient to our parents. I can recall that as a young boy of about ten George had a lot of friends in the neighborhood. One of the memories I have of him is how he liked to dress up and play cowboys. Dad had bought him a complete cowboy set: hat, belt with holster, gun, and some chaps. It was hard to get him out of this outfit.

George would help Dad out in the music shop. At a young age he was a natural storekeeper. As George grew up he would be sent out to sell our music books at the Star Theater or Sweets Ballroom, taking the books about the Mexican entertainer who was performing that day. George was the best salesman. He knew how to sell all his music books. He would work his way into the stars' rooms to meet them and get his books autographed.

George, like the rest of us, attended St. Mary's School. As the years went by he participated in many school activities. He was a good student, obedient and helping the sisters and priests in parish projects. This was George. He loved to help the parish. I talked to our newspaper collection man, Radio, about letting George have a newspaper corner on Broadway. He got a corner at Fourteenth Street in front of the Kress department store. The corner was a good one. Being the kind of guy looking for something to sell with paper, he came up with selling comic books. George would buy his books on Seventh Street at the shop between Washington Street and Broadway. Then he would sell them on his corner for ten cents. George became good friends with Radio, who would pick up all the boys in his REO truck to pay us our money. George would have Mom prepare dinner for his new friend Radio and his wife. We nicknamed George "Twenty Bucks." All his business transactions always seemed to profit him twenty dollars. At his age of twelve, this was good money. Mom once said to me that George was very active in the parish church, helping out so much that she worried about him getting sick from working too hard. George had said to her that he would like to go to the seminary to be a priest. Mom said that they could not afford this expense of schooling. I know George had set his goal on this calling. He took this as a big disappointment in his life.

George did work at odd jobs after leaving school. Mom and Dad rented him a room in back of the music shop. It had a separate entrance and was very small, just right for one person. He lived there until the new freeway came along and they tore down the old house. George then moved out to a friend's place toward the Oakland Mole, down Seventh Street heading west. By this time George had taken up drinking heavily. He lost his direction and the goals he set for himself at a young age. He did not care about anything else. Today George lives in a convalescent home in Hayward, in poor health.

Victor Llamas

My brother Victor, the youngest of the boys in my family, was born in July 1942 in Oakland, California. Being the youngest son, he was spoiled and allowed to get away with a lot. Mom and Dad both allowed this behavior. Victor was a very good-looking kid and had a good personality to go along with his good looks. As a young kid Victor always made friends with the local neighborhood kids. Growing up he did not have to help in the music shop as I, Eva, Mario, and George did. We learned a lot in helping Dad in the shop. Victor did not get this experience. In the 1950s he attended St. Mary's School for his early education and religious learning. Mom and Dad had moved to San Lorenzo for a new change. The house was larger and in a quiet neighborhood. Victor attended San Lorenzo High School where he made new friends. His new friends had the same beliefs as he did: they wanted no responsibilities.

The time was now the rock and roll era. He dressed with the current fashion of T-shirt and Levi's. He combed his black wavy hair with the curl at the front, the Tony Curtis look. He was part of the James Dean rebel era. Mom said his teenage years were rough on her and Dad. But I would tell her that all parents at this time were going through this new rock and roll period. The World War II babies had grown up, and they had fewer of the hardships that we endured. They lived now only for the good times.

Victor did work for Anita's Uncle George in his business selling flower corsages at the local dance halls and bars. Uncle George had established routes for the kids like my brother to sell corsages on the weekends, and would pay them very well. They earned a commission from the flower sales. They traveled to all the music dance halls and the larger dance bars in San Mateo, San Jose, Oakland, and Sacramento. This new responsibility of having a job did help him to grow up. At seventeen he also worked with his cousin Ronnie at the Bow and Bell restaurant at Jack London Square. They both were two good-looking kids and made impressive employees. Victor worked at Lady's Choice, a food company, and at the Port of Oakland as a dockworker. Victor lived through the 1960s hippie movement and the 1970s rock and roll period. He enjoyed his life to the fullest with no pressures. Victor is now living in Hayward, thinking back perhaps of all the good times he had.

Juanita Llamas

My sister Juanita was born July 1944 in Oakland, California. Juanita was the youngest in our family. She was a very cute child and an attractive girl growing up. She attended St. Mary's School on Seventh Street across from Jefferson Park. Being the youngest, Juanita received a lot of attention from all her siblings. Juanita was a good child. She always had a friendly happy smile for everyone. The shop was her playground; she grew up in the music shop. Being young, she was known by all the customers. In the early 1950s La Ideal Music Shop was busy with old-style Mexican music, the new Latin beats, and the mambo. This was a good time to be growing up, listening to the new music sounds plus rock and roll. Juanita was a smart girl. She helped Dad a lot with the shop business.

In the 1960s Juanita married Sam Salas. They had three daughters: Pamela, Giezell, and Michelle. She lived in East Oakland during her marriage. Juanita divorced Sam in the late 1960s. This was a big problem for her with three young children. She became a single mom. She overcame this setback and moved ahead with her life. She got through this detour and she now lives in San Leandro, enjoying her children and grandchildren.

Danny Cheveres (July 22, 1937–March 30, 1981)

Danny and I met in 1943 at Tompkins Elementary School where we became friends. I was six years old. The school is in West Oakland at Third Street and Adeline Street. Danny lived on Myrtle Street with his parents, Antonio and Isabel, and his sisters: Benita, Chaney, Cecelia, and Irene. I always remember his sisters. They were good-looking and fun to be around. This Puerto Rican family was very close to each other and showed their love for each other.

Being the only boy in the family, Danny was spoiled by the girls. Danny and I somehow ended up in the second grade together at St. Mary's School after our year together at Tompkins. Danny throughout our grade school years was always taller than me. I could never get ahead of the two inches that he always had on me. I remember our teacher, Sister Mary Frances, putting Danny in charge of the recess time in the schoolyard, responsible for keeping all the boys and girls behaving. I guess he always looked older, being taller than the rest of us.

Danny, along with Ron Houseman and me, was an altar boy for St. Mary's Church. This shared experience helped us become good friends as the years passed. Around 1949 we would hang out at his mom and dad's house on Myrtle Street. I must have been eleven years old. We would meet up with friends and ride our bikes through the neighborhood. Danny's parents were good to all us kids. His dad was a self-educated man who would give us kids good advice. He impressed me as a solid man, with his height of five feet seven inches, light reddish hair, very light skin, and blue eyes. He looked more Swedish than Puerto Rican. Danny's mom was an attractive lady. She made the best ham hocks with beans Puerto Rican-style with white rice.

Danny and I would sometimes hang out at St. Mary's clubhouse, which had been built in the school's basement under the class-rooms. The space was large and we had a boxing ring, pool tables, and a weight gym. We also spent lots of time riding our bikes. If we did not ride to the Point at the end of Seventh Street toward the San Francisco Bay Bridge, we might ride all over town, going through the Posey Tube toward Alameda. We also played a lot of baseball and kick the can in the street. Because Danny lived so close to the train tracks, we would go down and ride the slow trains to the Point. I think back on this and realize it was very unsafe. But at our age it seemed a lot of fun. Perhaps our freedom to do these things helped us know instinctively how to do them safely. The bike rides would include places further away like Lake Temescal, the Point, and many other interesting places in the Oakland area.

During our times together we also spent time thinking what we would do when we grew up. We saw lots of different things that people did. Danny and I visited the carnivals, the circus, the Oaks Ballpark, the midget car races, the boxing matches, and the activi-ties on Broadway. Somewhere in the 1950s, Danny bought a 1935 Ford sedan. He fixed it up using money he got from his summer job at a box factory putting together wooden boxes. The car, with the money from his job, gave him his independence. As his good buddy I also benefitted because now we had a car to go places.

By the middle of the 1950s Danny, now eighteen years old, wanted to join the Air Force. By this time I had new friends from high school and was seeing Anita, but I still missed Danny when he left for the Air Force. In the meanwhile, my brother Mario was dating Danny's sister, Cecelia. Danny returned from the service, and Mario and Cecelia married. Now I was happy to be part of the Cheveres family. Danny and I would meet sometimes and talk of old times. We never lost contact.

Danny married and started a family. I became godfather to this first child, Danny Junior. He became godfather to my son Stephen. Danny was now working for PG&E. I was working for PayLess. We had remained in close contact all through the years even though our lives and jobs changed how often we met. Then tragically he was gone. Danny died in a work-related accident with a PG&E work crew on March 30, 1981. I still remember him riding his bike and making the sign of the cross when we passed in front of St. Mary's Church. Once I asked him why he did this. He responded, "I respect God's house." So I began to do the same thing when passing the church. Danny was a good man, a man of faith, and a faithful friend. His wife Eva and daughter Isabel are the only survivors of Danny and Eva's family: their son, Danny Junior, and their third child, Adam, are also deceased.

Ron Houseman

Ron Houseman and I met around 1945 at Saint Mary's School on Seventh Street across from Jefferson Park. We were in the second grade with many other kids our age. Ron, as I remember back some sixty-six years, was a small kid with blonde hair, very light skin, tons of freckles on his face, and a lot of energy. I can remember Ron in grade school being very smart. He was a quick thinker and always wanted to please his friends. The kids in our school all had uniforms with light blue shirts, pepper-pot brown cords, and dark shoes. I was always impressed with Ron's shirts. His mom must have starched and ironed his shirts daily for school. Of all the kids I can remember, Ron stood out. Some of the other kids in this class were Albert Mammola, Paul and Olivia Duran, Gary Svihula, Vangie Cruz, Dolores Villa, Clara Baca, Danny Cheveres, Esther Chin, Remegio, James Kintrel, Tony Valdivia, Tommy Juarez, and Jean Harshman. Ron was from South Dakota, arriving in Oakland. He lived on Eighth and Brush Street, around the corner from me.

Ron was a newspaper boy like I was. He delivered the *Post Enquirer.* I sold newspapers on the corner of Tenth and Broadway. As boys we roamed all throughout West Oakland on our bikes with the other guys. Ron had a Schwinn bicycle. This bike had all the goodies: a battery tank for the front light, horn, and the special shocks on the front. This was the Cadillac of bikes in our time. I remember Ron leaving our school in the late part of 1949. He and his parents moved to Sunnyvale, California, on the other side of San Francisco Bay. I lost track of Ron for a time. But in the 1970s I relocated to Mountain View with my PayLess Drug Stores job. I was able to connect with Ron, who was working in real estate for Raintree Realtors, and later for his own company, Orchard Valley Realtors, and doing well. I had the pleasure of seeing his parents and visiting. We talked of West Oakland, our school, our friends, and our experiences as kids. We recalled the active times in West Oakland, especially before, during, and after World War II. The list of memories is long: Saint Mary's, Jefferson Park, the estuary at the bottom of Broadway, the department stores (Capwell's, Kahn's, Hale's) with their interesting window displays at Christmastime, especially the Lionel trains running around the scenes and items for sale. We also remembered Crabby Joe's Big Barn, the Big Western Bar, and the dancing and drinking, especially when the sailors, marines, and army guys were around. We recalled the Moulin Rouge Burlesque Theater with their poster pictures outside the lobby; Chinatown with twenty-five cent firecrackers and ladyfingers that we loved to explode for Fourth of July or other celebrations. Ron also remembered, as I do, the rides in the police paddy wagon when they took us to city baseball games. One special memory really stands out: when World War II was over everybody celebrated, cheering and dancing everywhere, even out on Broadway. Who could forget the creamery on Seventh Street? And sadly we remember the death of our grade school friend, Chebo. All these memories show our activity and bonds as a strong community.

Ron moved in 1978 to Vancouver, Washington. I have kept in touch with him. He is still sharp and selling real estate while I am writing my memoir. We are not the boomers, but I guess we could be called the "Do It" generation. We were always doing something, and many of us still keep going, from our humble start in West Oakland in this great country of ours. We learned to treat all people with respect. We might have been ignorant of local wrongs and discriminations in Oakland in general. But as individuals we tried to respect those we met, to go about our business with honesty and loyalty, and live life as it came to us.

Antonio Armando Valdivia

Tony Valdivia is my dear boyhood friend. We grew up together in West Oakland in a Mexican immigrant community prior to and during World War II. We attended St. Mary's School across from Jefferson Park on Seventh Street. I met Tony in the second grade. Our teachers, who belonged to the Holy Name Sisters, were stern taskmasters, as many nuns were at that time. We learned the basic essential subjects and how to pray. I was an altar boy with Tony. I can remember sitting with Tony learning the Latin prayers and responses we had to recite during Mass. This memory stands out as a special event in our lives. Tony's parents were great and hardworking people. One of the restaurants they owned was El Rio Grande Mexican restaurant on Seventh Street, feeding the locals and the braceros. In school, Tony was very smart. At times he would join our group of kids playing volleyball during recess at school. One of the things I recall of Tony is his hardy, happy, and strong laugh, which he still has.

When we completed the eighth grade, Tony had already left Oakland to attend the seminary for his education to be a priest. Tommy Juarez did the same. (I lost track of Tommy.) I have followed Tony's priestly career through people I know in West Oakland. Tony's being a priest seems an interesting career. He has had assignments all over the Bay Area and even out of the country. Tony was ordained April 6, 1963, in Oakland, California.

Tony's assignments have included serving as associate pastor at Our Lady of Grace, Castro Valley (1963–1967), and St. Bernard's, Oakland (1967–1971); as priest in residence at St. Clement's, Hayward, and graduate student California State–Hayward in guidance counseling (1971–1976); and as pastor at St. Anthony's, Oakland (1976–1986), St. Leonard's, Fremont (1986–1991), St. Cornelius, Richmond (1993–2001), St. Catherine of Siena,

Martinez (2001–2003), and St. Louis Bertrand, Oakland (2003–2007). He also attended college and retreats and took a sabbatical in Louvain, Belgium (1986), and performed missionary work in Santa Lucia, Ilopongo, San Salvador, El Salvador (1991–1993).

Tony is now a monsignor, still working in the Diocese of Oakland. Tony has a strong work ethic that his parents instilled in him at a young age along with the strong love for all his people.

A Llamas family event, 2006. Front: Wally, Anita, and Ruben; back, Willie, Mario Jr. (Ruben's nephew), and Steve.

Ruben and Monsignor Tony Valdivia at the Oakland Cathedral, 2009.

Bibliography

Cox, Gerald F. *The Radical Peasant.* Canada: Trafford Publishing, 2006.

Krell, Dorothy, ed. *The California Missions: A Pictorial History.* 7th printing. Menlo Park, Calif.: Sunset Publishing Corporation, 1993.

Massey, Douglas S., Durand, Jorge, and Malone, Nolan J. *Beyond Smoke and Mirrors: Mexican Immigration in an Era of Economic Integration.* New York: Russell Sage Foundation, 2002.

Stone, Adolf, ed. *California Information Almanac.* California State Series. Sacramento: California State Department of Education, 1965.

Trimble, Paul C. *Images of Rail: Railways of San Francisco.* Charleston, SC: Arcadia Publishing, 2004.

Trimble, Paul C. *Interurban Railways of the Bay Area.* Fresno, Calif.: Valley Publishers, 1977.